OXFORD
UNIVERSITY PRESS

Blackstone's Police Investigators
Mock Examination Paper 2024

Pack 1

Contents

AF729295

OXFORD
UNIVERSITY PRESS

Great Clarendon Street, Oxford, OX2 6DP,
United Kingdom

Oxford University Press is a department of the University of Oxford.
It furthers the University's objective of excellence in research, scholarship,
and education by publishing worldwide. Oxford is a registered trade mark of
Oxford University Press in the UK and in certain other countries

First Edition published in 2004
Twentieth Edition published in 2023

Published in the United States of America by Oxford University Press
198 Madison Avenue, New York, NY 10016, United States of America

British Library Cataloguing in Publication Data
Data available

Library of Congress Control Number
Data available

ISBN 978–0–19–889134–5

DOI: 10.1093/law/9780198891345.001.0001

Printed in the UK by
Bell & Bain Ltd., Glasgow

Acknowledgements

Thanks to all the staff at Oxford University Press, particularly Fiona Briden and Jordan Burke. I would like to thank Dave Pinfield for his contributions to this Mock Examination.

Paul Connor

Introduction to the Mock Examination

Some students taking the National Investigators' Examination (NIE) have never sat an examination of this type—some may have had the experience of taking the Sergeants' and/or Inspectors' promotion examination. Regardless of the position a student is in, preparation for the NIE can be daunting as it involves having to study a significant amount of text often in a short time frame (14 weeks or less); this is far more intense than either the Sergeants' or Inspectors' examinations.

To assist your preparation, you can obtain multiple-choice questions (MCQs) from a variety of different sources. The Blackstone's online MCQ database is an excellent resource and is available via Oxford University Press. It contains a large database of multiple-choice questions, based directly on the content of the *Blackstone's Police Investigators' Manual*, and you can find more information here: http://www.blackstonespoliceservice.com/. The *Blackstone's Police Investigators' Q&A* is also available and contains in excess of 400 questions specifically designed for the NIE student. But whilst these are helpful and assist in testing your knowledge, taking a mock examination is a different type of experience. Whilst it is impossible to recreate the exact same environment and MCQs you will face in the exam, taking this mock is a useful exercise—for example:

- It might highlight an issue with time management.
- Answering 80 MCQs is not a routine experience—simply completing the mock helps your preparation.
- It may identify strengths/weaknesses in your knowledge.

To make this mock experience as realistic as possible, it will follow the structure of an 'average' NIE as closely as possible. The first point to make here is that the examination contains 80 MCQs, 10 of which will not count towards your overall mark. These 10 MCQs are those that perform poorly against a broad range of criteria (*the sole criteria* these questions are judged against *is not* how many candidates answer the MCQ incorrectly). As analysing future candidate performance in relation to the 80 MCQs in this mock to obtain such data is not possible, 10 MCQs have been randomly selected to count as those 'poor performing' MCQs to ensure that you are marked out of 70.

The content of the MCQs in your examination is based solely on the content of the *Blackstone's Investigators' Manual 2024* and the four sections it contains (General Principles, Police Powers and Procedures; Serious Crime and Other Offences; Property Offences; and Sexual Offences) so the content of other resources has zero relevance to this mock exam.

An analysis of the structure of examinations held over the last three years shows that the 'average' NIE consists of 30 MCQs on General Principles, Police Powers and Procedures, 16 MCQs on Serious Crime and Other Offences, 12 MCQs on Property Offences and 12 on Sexual Offences (the 70 MCQs that count towards your mark). Recent examinations (in 2023) have shown a slight shift from Property Offences and Sexual Offences to Serious Crime and Other Offences—so this mock will follow a similar structure (including the 10 random MCQs that, for marking purposes, will be considered as 'poor performing' MCQs).

A significant change in the presentation of MCQs in your exam is that they are now presented in the order of the four parts of the Manual (although not in chapter order). Mirroring that exam structure means that you will begin this mock by answering 36 randomly ordered MCQs on General Principles, Police Powers and Procedures followed by 22 randomly ordered MCQs on Serious Crime and Other Offences etc.

There can be no guarantee that this will represent the precise structure of your NIE in terms of content but the mock exam does draw from almost every chapter in the Manual at some stage so it will provide you with an opportunity to test yourself against the broad spectrum of the syllabus.

Since September 2020, the College of Policing has reserved the right to change the pass mark in the NIE *if* there is a significant variance in the pass rate of exams that are taken 'online' compared to the previous format (on paper). After each exam, the debrief panel will consider whether it is appropriate to change the exam pass mark to ensure assessment standards are in line with previous years. To date, this has not happened and, as this is a factor that is entirely out of your control, it would be sensible to set your target at 55.71% (a 'pass') but the better your score, the more likely you will be successful even if the College does consider it appropriate to raise the pass mark (it is also possible that the mark could be lowered, of course). To score 55.71%, you will need to answer 39 out of 70 questions correctly (each correct answer is worth 1.42%).

I wish you all the very best in this mock examination.

Paul Connor

Instructions for Completion

READ THE WHOLE OF THE INSTRUCTIONS BEFORE ATTEMPTING THE MOCK EXAMINATION

If you want to get the most from this mock examination, then you must treat it as if you were sitting the examination proper.

Time

You have up to two hours to complete the examination. It might not take you that long but it is best to assume that it will, so please make absolutely sure that you set aside two hours. You cannot expect to sit part of the examination for one hour, take a break for 20 minutes, return to the examination and then get an accurate picture of your performance—the examination must be completed in one two-hour sitting. However, if you have been allocated extra time to take the exam (for example, you may have been provided with reasonable adjustments because you are dyslexic), add that time to the standard two-hour exam time frame and if you include breaks, take them—the idea is that the mock exam is taken in the same circumstances as you would take the exam proper.

Environment

You need to be able to concentrate on the examination and you cannot do that if the television is on, the phone is ringing etc. Find a place where you will not be disturbed for the duration of this examination and make sure that there are no distractions that will affect your performance.

Make sure that you can see a clock, stopwatch or wristwatch.

You will need two pencils, a pencil sharpener and an eraser.

If you require any other materials in relation to reasonable adjustments, ensure they are available to you.

Pack 1

In Pack 1, you will find a blank answer sheet and the question booklet.

When you decide to start the examination, please open the question booklet. Work through the mock questions and make your choice of A, B, C or D by putting a horizontal line through the corresponding letter on the answer sheet.

Mark only one answer for each question.

Make sure that if you change your answer you erase the previous mark fully.

Pack 2

When you have finished the examination, open Pack 2 and begin the marking process. When you have finished marking your paper, please refer to the answer booklet for a detailed explanation of the correct answers with paragraph references to the *Blackstone's Police Investigators' Manual 2024*.

The marking process will take some time—to ensure accuracy; please do not rush this stage!

OXFORD
UNIVERSITY PRESS

Blackstone's Police Investigators' Mock Examination Paper 2024

Question Booklet

Time Allowed—120 minutes

1. Each of the questions is followed by four possible answers, only ONE of which is correct. Choose the ONE response that you consider to be correct. On the answer sheet, mark the box that corresponds to your selection. Mark your answer clearly with a — mark. The answer sheet has spaces for your answers to all questions. If you change your mind about an answer, rub out the first mark, then mark your new answer. Mark only one answer for each question.
2. You are reminded that there is no need to read the whole examination paper before beginning to select answers to the questions posed.
3. You must ensure that BEFORE the close of the examination all of your answers to the questions have been correctly entered on the answer sheet. If you leave a question unanswered for any reason, it will not receive a mark.
4. You may make any notes you wish on the question papers.

OXFORD
UNIVERSITY PRESS

Blackstone's Police Investigators' Mock Examination Paper 2024

Question Booklet

1. MARTINEZ (aged 16 years) is in custody at a designated police station after having been arrested for an offence of burglary (a recordable offence which is contrary to the Theft Act 1968). Non-intimate samples have not been obtained from MARTINEZ in the course of the investigation and DC GRAINGER, the officer in the case, now proposes to obtain those samples. MARTINEZ refuses to consent to the non-intimate samples being taken from him.

   Which of the statements below is correct in relation to the taking of non-intimate samples in such a situation?

   A As MARTINEZ is a juvenile, non-intimate samples cannot be obtained from him in this situation.
   B An officer of the rank of inspector or above must authorise the taking of a non-intimate sample from MARTINEZ.
   C A non-intimate sample cannot be taken from a detainee unless they provide written consent to the sample being taken.
   D A non-intimate sample can be taken from MARTINEZ by force as long as a record is made of the circumstances and those present at the time the sample is obtained.

2. RANKINE is accused of committing an offence of theft from his employer. PC DAVISON arranges for RANKINE to voluntarily attend a police station to be interviewed regarding the offence. RANKINE attends the police station accompanied by FINLEY (RANKINE's legal representative). The interview takes place and RANKINE leaves having been told by PC DAVISON that he may be required to attend court in relation to the theft. It is decided that RANKINE should be charged with the theft and appear at magistrates' court to answer the charge.

   In relation to the service of the written charge and requisition, which of the following comments is correct?

   A They must be handed personally to RANKINE or posted to him at an address where it is reasonably believed that RANKINE will receive them (they could not be served on FINLEY).
   B As RANKINE was legally represented, they must be served on FINLEY (they could not be served on RANKINE).
   C These documents could be served by handing them in person to RANKINE or to FINLEY.
   D The documents must be served physically (by handing them to RANKINE or FINLEY or being posted to an address where it is reasonably believed RANKINE or FINLEY will receive them); they cannot be served electronically.

3. GOWAN (who is 17 years old) is a witness to an offence of s. 18 wounding where the victim was stabbed with a knife. RUTHERFORD is arrested and charged with the offence and pleads 'not guilty' to it and a date has been set for the trial at Crown Court. GOWAN contacts the officer in the case, PC DEEN (who is also a witness in the case), and asks about the procedure in relation to her giving witness evidence in the Crown Court.

   Considering the law regarding special measures contained in the Youth Justice and Criminal Evidence Act 1999, which of the following comments is correct?

   A Regardless of the nature of the offence, GOWAN is eligible to give evidence by video interview and the use of live link, but if she wishes to do so, she can testify in the Crown Court.
   B GOWAN is automatically eligible for a special measures direction; PC DEEN would not be eligible for a special measures direction.
   C The primary rule is that all witnesses under the age of 18 must give their evidence via video interview and live link—a witness under the age of 18 is prohibited from testifying in Crown Court.
   D GOWAN would be eligible for special measures only if she were in fear or distress about testifying.

4. GOUGH commits an offence under s. 4 of the Public Order Act 1986 (fear or provocation of violence). PC MAHROOF (an officer in uniform) visits GOUGH's home address to speak with GOUGH. When GOUGH answers the front door and sees the officer, he shouts *'Fuck off!'* and slams the door in the officer's face. PC MAHROOF reasonably believes that GOUGH is still on the premises and is considering his powers of entry to effect an arrest.

   If PC MAHROOF considers it necessary to arrest GOUGH, could the officer enter and search the premises in order to arrest GOUGH using his powers of entry under s. 17 of the Police and Criminal Evidence Act 1984?

   A Yes, but this is only because the officer is in uniform.
   B No, as the offence under s. 4 of the Public Order Act 1986 is triable summarily only (it is not an indictable offence).
   C Yes, and force may be used in exercising the power where it is necessary to do so.
   D No, as GOUGH is not unlawfully at large and PC MAHROOF is not in 'hot pursuit' of him.

5. DC SPURLING approaches her supervisor for some advice relating to covert human intelligence sources (CHIS). DC SPURLING has been approached by OTTER (aged 15 years) who has told the officer that he has high-quality information about the drug-dealing activities of his uncle (TURNER). TURNER lives 20 miles away from OTTER and his family but regularly visits OTTER's parents and boasts about how much money he is making from his drug-dealing activities. OTTER wants to provide the information to the police because he is disgusted by the behaviour of his uncle.

   Could OTTER be authorised as a CHIS in these circumstances?

   A Yes, although the authorisation would be for a maximum of one month (beginning on the day the authorisation was granted).
   B No, as a child under the age of 16 cannot be authorised to carry out CHIS activity in any circumstances.
   C Yes, although the authorisation would be for a maximum of four months (beginning on the day the authorisation was granted).
   D No, as the conduct of a juvenile CHIS cannot involve that CHIS providing information about any member of his/her family.

6. SHEFFIELD is attacked and robbed by TAYLOR (who is a stranger to SHEFFIELD). DC McCUBBIN is first to arrive at the scene of the offence and quickly obtains a first description of TAYLOR from SHEFFIELD. DC McCUBBIN places SHEFFIELD in an unmarked police vehicle and drives SHEFFIELD around the local area to see if he can identify the person responsible for the offence. They drive along a busy street with a cafe on one side of the road and a pub on the other. People are outside both premises and SHEFFIELD is looking intently at a group outside the cafe. DC McCUBBIN sees a person who matches the description given by SHEFFIELD standing outside the pub with a group of people and asks SHEFFIELD to look closely at the group outside the pub. As a result, SHEFFIELD identifies TAYLOR who is in the group outside the pub and is subsequently arrested by other officers searching the area.

   In relation to Code D of the Codes of Practice, which of the following comments is correct?

   A Code D has not been complied with as once a first description of an offender has been obtained from an eyewitness they should not take part in any 'street' identification process.
   B Code D has not been complied with as DC McCUBBIN is not allowed to draw the attention of SHEFFIELD to a particular group.
   C Code D has not been complied with as at least two officers must be present when such a 'street' identification process takes place.
   D Code D of the Codes of Practice has been complied with by the officer.

7. WILSON has been arrested for drug-related crimes. At the custody block, the arresting officer informs the custody sergeant that there is evidence that WILSON has swallowed some drugs. WILSON's detention is authorised and the officers wish to carry out an X-ray or ultrasound scan on WILSON.

In order to comply with s. 55A of PACE 1984, which of the following statements is correct?

A The drug swallowed must be a Class A and have been for supply or export. The authority required is that of an inspector and force can be used.
B The drug swallowed must be a Class A drug and have been for supply or export. The authority required is that of an inspector (along with the consent of WILSON) and no force can be used.
C The drug swallowed can be a Class A, B or C and have been for supply or export. The authority required is that of an inspector (along with the consent of WILSON) and no force can be used.
D The drug swallowed can be a Class A, B or C and have been for supply or export. The authority required is that of an inspector and force can be used.

8. SHEWARD is a member of a gang which is responsible for a series of robberies. SHEWARD is arrested at the scene of the gang's latest robbery but the other members of the gang manage to escape. SHEWARD is taken to a designated police station where he requests that his friend, BUCKLER, is informed of his arrest. The arresting officer, DC DOVEY, believes that BUCKLER is the person who handles the stolen goods from the robberies and that informing BUCKLER of SHEWARD's arrest will hinder the recovery of property from the robberies. DC DOVEY wishes to delay SHEWARD's exercise of this right.

Which of the statements below is correct?

A The delay can be authorised by an inspector. The maximum period of the delay is 36 hours.
B The delay can be authorised by an inspector. The maximum period of the delay is 48 hours.
C The delay must be authorised by a superintendent. The maximum period of the delay is 36 hours.
D The delay must be authorised by a superintendent. The maximum period of the delay is 48 hours.

9. ABDULLAHI has attended a designated police station voluntarily to be interviewed regarding an offence of assault. ABDULLAHI arrived at the police station at 13.30 hours and was arrested for the offence at 14.00 hours. He has been interviewed about the offence and began an eight-hour rest period at 22.00 hours. At 23.30 hours, ABDULLAHI's solicitor requested a consultation with him which was allowed to take place by the custody officer, PS FREER.

   In relation to ABDULLAHI's eight-hour rest period, which of the following comments is correct?

   A ABDULLAHI's rest period should not have been interrupted at the request of his legal representative.
   B A fresh eight-hour period for rest is not required once the consultation is concluded.
   C In any period of 24 hours, a detainee must be allowed a continuous period of at least eight hours for rest—in ABDULLAHI's case, the period of 24 hours runs from the time of his arrival at the police station.
   D ABDULLAHI's rest period can only be interrupted where there are reasonable grounds for believing that not interrupting it would involve a risk of harm to people or serious loss of, or damage to, property.

10. CRUIKSHANK has been arrested for an offence of violent disorder and is being interviewed about the offence at a designated police station—the interview is being visually recorded. CRUIKSHANK is legally represented in the interview by his solicitor. The interviewing officers ask a number of questions of CRUIKSHANK during the interview but he remains completely silent having been told to do so by his solicitor who has told the interviewing officers that he has advised his client to do so in response to all questions put to him in interview. CRUIKSHANK genuinely relies on the advice of his solicitor to remain silent.

    Could adverse inferences (under s. 34 of the Criminal Justice and Public Order Act 1994) be drawn from CRUIKSHANK's failure to respond to questions in the interview?

    A No, CRUIKSHANK's genuine reliance on the advice of his solicitor to stay silent is not, in itself, enough to preclude adverse inferences.
    B Yes, CRUIKSHANK could be convicted solely on an inference drawn from silence.
    C No, adverse inferences can only be drawn from an interview where the defendant responds to questioning; they cannot be drawn from an interview where the defendant remains silent.
    D Yes, adverse inferences may be drawn from CRUIKSHANK's silence but only because he was legally represented during the course of the interview.

11. GUNNEL and PLEYDEN agree to steal a Ferrari motor vehicle from a garage selling specialist vehicles. The plan is that GUNNEL will act as a 'look out' outside the garage while PLEYDEN breaks in and steals the car. On the evening of the offence, things are going to plan when PLEYDEN is disturbed in the garage by HENDERSON, a security guard. PLEYDEN produces a knuckleduster and assaults HENDERSON, causing him extremely serious injury in the process. The fact that PLEYDEN was in possession of a knuckleduster was unknown to GUNNEL who was only committed to stealing the Ferrari and nothing else.

With regard to the law that deals with principals and accessories, which of the following comments is correct?

A The fact that GUNNEL is present at the scene of the offence when it is committed, in itself, amounts to encouragement that would support a charge making him an accessory to the offence against HENDERSON.
B GUNNEL is liable for the injury to HENDERSON as GUNNEL and PLEYDEN have embarked on a 'joint enterprise', meaning that each person is liable for the actions of the other.
C GUNNEL is not liable for the serious injuries caused to HENDERSON as PLEYDEN has done something that has gone beyond what was agreed.
D In order for an accessory to be liable for the actions of the principal, the accessory must physically take part in the offence (in this case, the harm caused to HENDERSON) and, as that is not the case here, GUNNEL is not liable for the injury to HENDERSON.

12. MILEY is 15 years old and has been arrested for an offence of theft. The custody officer, PS SESAY, makes contact with MILEY's biological father who arrives at the police station 30 minutes after the contact from PS SESAY was made. MILEY expressly and specifically refuses to have his biological father act as an appropriate adult as he is estranged from him, the last contact between the two being over three years earlier. MILEY's biological father is told of this but demands that he is allowed to look after his son's welfare.

What should happen in these circumstances?

A The custody officer can allow MILEY's father to act as an appropriate adult in this situation.
B As MILEY expressly and specifically objects to the presence of his biological father, his father should not be asked to act as the appropriate adult.
C An officer of the rank of inspector or above would have to authorise the exclusion of MILEY's biological father.
D MILEY's biological father must be allowed to act as the appropriate adult.

13. MASON was arrested for an offence of robbery. Whilst in police detention, his fingerprints were taken and he was later bailed for further enquiries to be made in relation to the offence. It is subsequently discovered that the fingerprints obtained from MASON were not of sufficient quality to allow satisfactory analysis to take place.

In relation to a requirement for MASON to attend a police station to have his fingerprints taken, which of the following comments is correct?

A MASON can be required to attend a police station for his fingerprints to be obtained, although no power of arrest exists should he decline to attend.
B If there is an urgent need for MASON's fingerprints to be obtained for the purposes of the investigation of the offence, an officer of the rank of inspector or above may authorise a period shorter than seven days for MASON to attend the police station.
C MASON should be given a period of at least 14 days within which to attend a police station to have his fingerprints taken.
D MASON cannot be required to attend a police station for an additional set of fingerprints to be taken unless he has been charged or reported for an offence.

14. KHATUN has been charged with an offence of attempted rape and the issue of bail is now being considered. KHATUN has a previous conviction for manslaughter, for which he served five years' imprisonment (that manslaughter conviction is 12 years old) and he has no other previous convictions.

Will the provisions of s. 25 of the Criminal Justice and Public Order Act 1994 be applicable in these circumstances?

A Yes, as KHATUN will not be granted bail unless there are exceptional circumstances which justify it.
B No, as KHATUN's previous conviction for manslaughter is over 10 years old.
C Yes, due to the nature of the charge and because of KHATUN's previous conviction, he cannot be granted bail.
D No, as s. 25 only relates to defendants charged with murder, attempted murder or manslaughter.

15. A large number of burglaries at commercial premises have taken place and goods to the value of £2 million pounds have been stolen. An operation is commenced in relation to the offences leading to the arrest of CALDERDALE who is later charged with the burglary offences. Sergeant WARWICK is the disclosure officer in the case and is liaising with his Professional Standards Department as to whether information regarding allegations of, and the misconduct of, several officers involved in the investigation should be revealed to the prosecutor.

Considering the Disclosure Code of Practice and advice given to prosecutors by the DPP, which of the following comments is correct?

A Sergeant WARWICK will have the final responsibility for the value judgement on whether information relating to misconduct of police officers should be revealed to the prosecutor.
B Findings in relation to disciplinary matters, regardless of their nature, must always be revealed to the prosecution which must, in turn, disclose them to the defence.
C There is no duty on the prosecution to disclose details of unsubstantiated complaints against a police officer.
D Disciplinary matters are not criminal convictions and consequently have no relevance as far as disclosure is concerned.

16. PRASAD has been arrested in connection with an offence of attempted kidnapping. The victim states that when PRASAD tried to kidnap her, he was not wearing a top of any description and she managed to scratch him on the chest with her fingernails. The victim states that the scratches were deep and left four large marks on the left side of PRASAD's chest. The officer in the case, DS JACKSON, wishes to examine PRASAD under s. 54A of the Police and Criminal Evidence Act 1984 (as amended by the Anti-terrorism, Crime and Security Act 2001), to ascertain whether or not he has such marks on his chest as their presence would tend to identify him as the person involved in the commission of the offence.

Which of the following statements is correct?

A The custody officer can authorise that PRASAD be examined without his consent but this must be authorised in writing.
B PRASAD can be examined for the presence of the marks but only if he consents and an officer of the rank of inspector or above authorises the examination.
C PRASAD cannot be examined as the Act allows only for the search and/or examination of an individual to establish their identification and not for evidence in relation to the offence for which they have been arrested.
D An inspector must authorise the examination; authorisation can be given orally or in writing.

17. PC OZDEMIR has arrested PEARCE in relation to an offence of robbery. The officer is putting together an interview plan which involves consideration of what information to make available to PEARCE's solicitor, CARTER. PC OZDEMIR approaches you, as her supervisor, for some advice regarding what should be disclosed to a solicitor prior to the interview with PEARCE. The officer is unsure about whether the custody record and an initial description given by a witness of the offender (the 'first description') should be disclosed.

Must both or either of these items be disclosed to CARTER before the interview with PEARCE takes place?

A Yes, the custody record and the record of 'first description' must be provided to CARTER before PEARCE is interviewed about the offence.
B No, there is no provision within the Police and Criminal Evidence Act 1984 or the Codes of Practice for the disclosure of any information by the police at the police station.
C Yes, the custody record must be disclosed.
D No, although if these items are not disclosed then no inference could be drawn by a court from PEARCE's silence.

18. FISHER has attended a designated police station at the request of PC JAKEMAN to take part in a voluntary interview regarding an allegation of theft. It is PC JAKEMAN's intention that the interview will be audio recorded but when FISHER arrives at the police station, the two interview rooms at the police station are unavailable (one of the rooms has a fault with the recording equipment and the other is being used to interview a suspect and will not be available for some time).

If a written record of the interview is to be made, who would be the 'relevant officer' in these circumstances?

A An officer of the rank of inspector or above.
B The custody officer at the designated police station.
C PC JAKEMAN (the interviewing officer).
D An officer of the rank of sergeant or above.

19. OGINSKY (aged 16 years) has been arrested for an offence of robbery (a recordable offence) and has been transported to the custody block of a designated police station. DC PIGDEN (the officer in the case) interviews OGINSKY in the presence of FARROW (who is OGINSKY's uncle and acting as an appropriate adult). During the interview, DC PIGDEN tells OGINSKY that he wishes to obtain footwear impressions from him (under s. 61A of the Police and Criminal Evidence Act 1984) and asks for his consent—OGINSKY refuses.

    Can DC PIGDEN obtain footwear samples from OGINSKY in these circumstances?

    A No, as footwear samples can only be obtained from a person in police detention with their written consent.
    B Yes, and DC PIGDEN can use force to obtain them if necessary.
    C No, unless FARROW provides written consent for DC PIGDEN to obtain footwear impressions from OGINSKY.
    D Yes, if the impressions are necessary to prove or disprove OGINSKY's involvement in the robbery offence.

20. FLACK had a short relationship with STIRLING but STIRLING broke up with FLACK. FLACK wants revenge against STIRLING and wishes to cause him problems but is scared of doing anything herself, so she encourages BEST to cause criminal damage to a VW Golf car owned by STIRLING. BEST agrees and visits STIRLING's house. He sees a VW Golf outside STIRLING's house and slashes all the tyres with a knife but he has made a mistake as the car does not belong to STIRLING—it belongs to DUTTON. DUTTON sees BEST damaging his car and confronts BEST. In the struggle that follows, BEST commits a s. 39 battery offence (contrary to the Criminal Justice Act 1988) against DUTTON.

    In relation to the criminal damage and the battery, would the doctrine of transferred *mens rea* apply to FLACK in these circumstances?

    A Yes, but FLACK would only be liable as an accessory to the criminal damage to DUTTON's car.
    B No, the doctrine has no applicability in this situation as it is only relevant when considering offences against the person under the Offences Against the Person Act 1861.
    C Yes, FLACK is liable as an accessory to the criminal damage and s. 39 battery offence.
    D No, transferred *mens rea* does not apply to FLACK as he is an accessory—the doctrine only has applicability when considering the actions of a principal offender.

21. PC ARROW is directed to attend a call where it is reported that a person is behaving suspiciously around some farm buildings. The officer arrives at the scene and sees PURLEY walking out of a farm building and across a field. There is a very large sign next to the field indicating that it is private property. As PURLEY climbs over a fence and into the road, PC ARROW stops him. PURLEY admits he was looking for somewhere to sleep for the night and was trespassing. The officer searches PURLEY and finds an air pistol in his possession. PC ARROW arrests PURLEY in respect of his commission of an offence of trespassing with a firearm on land (contrary to s. 20(2) of the Firearms Act 1968 and using the provisions of s. 24 of the Police and Criminal Evidence Act 1984). PC ARROW now wishes to use the provisions of s. 32 of the Police and Criminal Evidence Act 1984 to search PURLEY and the nearby farm building.

With regard to the officer's powers under s. 32 of the Police and Criminal Evidence Act 1984, which of the following comments is true?

A PC ARROW cannot search the farm building that PURLEY was seen walking out from under s. 32 of the Act.
B PC ARROW has a power under s. 32 to search PURLEY for evidence but only for evidence specifically relating to the offence for which he was arrested.
C PC ARROW may require PURLEY to remove his outer coat, jacket and gloves for the purpose of the search but he cannot search in PURLEY's mouth.
D If PC ARROW suspects that PURLEY may present a danger to himself or others, then he may search him.

22. PC CROSSFIELD attends the scene of a theft of cash from an office block. When the officer walks into the office, she is approached by LINTON who states, '*Officer, I stole the money. I want to confess.*' LINTON is arrested for theft and taken to a designated police station. PC CROSSFIELD records the comment made by LINTON as soon as practicable, noting when it was made and signing it in her pocket book.

Which of the following comments is correct regarding the comment made by LINTON to PC CROSSFIELD?

A It is a 'significant statement' and it should be put to LINTON at the beginning of the interview with him, after caution and before questioning.
B It is not a 'significant statement' as it was made at an office block rather than at a designated police station.
C It is a 'significant statement' and it should be put to LINTON at the conclusion of any interview with him and at the end of questioning.
D It is not a 'significant statement' as it was not made in response to and after any form of caution.

23. BROWN has been charged with an offence of burglary and has been bailed by PS KING (the custody officer). PS KING imposed a number of bail conditions on BROWN, including a curfew between set times. One week after being bailed, BROWN finds out that his girlfriend is pregnant and wants to have his bail condition of curfew modified so that he can help his girlfriend during her pregnancy.

Which of the following comments is correct in respect of varying the bail condition?

A BROWN must speak to PS KING who is the only person who can vary the conditions of bail.
B BROWN's conditions of bail can be varied by PS KING or another custody officer serving at any police station in PS KING's force area.
C BROWN's conditions of bail can be varied by PS KING or another custody officer serving at the same police station that PS KING works at.
D BROWN's conditions of bail can be varied but only by a magistrates' court.

24. FELL (who is 18 years old) and SAYER (who is 17 years old) have been arrested in connection with an offence of robbery. The officer in charge of the case, DC HEINZMAN, has information and evidence that FELL and SAYER are responsible for a large number of other robbery offences and wishes to speak to them about these offences. As such, DC HEINZMAN seeks to have FELL and SAYER remanded into police custody under s. 128 of the Magistrates' Courts Act 1980 so that he can speak to them about the other robbery offences.

Which of the following comments is correct in relation to such a remand?

A FELL could be remanded in police custody for a period not exceeding three clear days; SAYER could not be remanded in police custody as he is a juvenile.
B FELL could be remanded in police custody for a period not exceeding three clear days; SAYER could be remanded in police custody for a period not exceeding 24 hours.
C FELL and SAYER could be remanded in police custody for a period not exceeding three clear days.
D FELL and SAYER could be remanded in police custody for a period not exceeding 24 hours.

25. LAPORT contacts DC VALENTINE with information in relation to a large shipment of drugs being moved in an articulated lorry. LAPORT works in a transport depot and states that he heard several of his work colleagues talking about the shipment and that they would finalise details at a meeting at the depot in approximately four hours' time. LAPORT tells DC VALENTINE that he can provide further information about the shipment to assist the police. In order to do so, DC VALENTINE requires urgent authorisation for LAPORT to act as a Covert Human Intelligence Source (CHIS).

In relation to such an 'urgent' CHIS authorisation, which of the following comments is correct?

A An officer of at least the rank of inspector can authorise 'urgent' CHIS activity; the authorisation must be given in writing and will last for 72 hours.
B An officer of at least the rank of inspector can authorise 'urgent' CHIS activity; the authorisation can be provided orally or in writing and will last for 24 hours.
C An officer of at least the rank of superintendent must authorise 'urgent' CHIS activity; the authorisation can be given orally or in writing and will last for 48 hours.
D An officer of at least the rank of superintendent must authorise 'urgent' CHIS activity; the authorisation can be given orally or in writing and will last for 96 hours.

26. BUSHNETT has been charged with an offence of assault (contrary to s. 47 of the Offences Against the Person Act 1861) and has been bailed by the police to make a first appearance at a magistrates' court in relation to the offence. BUSHNETT does not appear at court on that date and is later arrested for absconding (under s. 7 of the Bail Act 1976). When arrested, BUSHNETT states that he had a reasonable excuse for his failure to appear as he made a genuine error about his date of appearance at the magistrates' court; this came about because the police failed to give him a copy of the record of the decision to bail him (which included the date on which he was supposed to appear).

In relation to the offence under s. 6 of the Bail Act 1976 (offence of absconding by a person released on bail), which of the following comments is correct?

A BUSHNETT has a 'reasonable excuse' for his failure to appear (the failure by the police to provide him with a copy of the record of the decision).
B The offence under s. 6 would not be appropriate as this is limited to a situation where the person fails to appear at a court having been granted bail by a court (not 'police bail').
C The facts that BUSHNETT made a genuine error about his date of appearance and that the police did not give him a copy of the record of the bail decision are irrelevant; he has committed the offence in these circumstances.
D BUSHNETT has a 'reasonable excuse' for his failure to appear (the fact that he made a genuine error about his date of appearance).

27. MICHAM has been arrested in relation to an offence of robbery. He denies any involvement in the offence, disputing the identification evidence. MICHAM has indicated that he will not take part in any video identification or identification parade so consideration is being given to a group identification process.

Considering Annex C of Code D of the Codes of Practice (dealing with group identification), which of the following statements is correct?

A A group identification may only take place with MITCHAM's consent and cooperation.
B A group identification process can take place at a police station.
C A group identification process must involve a moving (not stationary) group.
D A group identification process must be video recorded in all circumstances.

28. CALLAGHAN drives onto the forecourt of a motorway service station and whilst filling his car with fuel sees RICE, a hitchhiker, holding a sign stating 'Lift to London?' CALLAGHAN is attracted to RICE and approaches her and states that he will give her a lift. RICE accepts and gets in to the front passenger seat of CALLAGHAN's car. CALLAGHAN drives off the forecourt onto the motorway. The two engage in conversation as CALLAGHAN drives along the slip road towards the motorway. Just before the vehicle joins the motorway, CALLAGHAN tells RICE *'Now I've got you, I'm going to fuck you whether you like it or not!'* and grabs hold of RICE's right breast. RICE is petrified and thinks she is going to be raped. She opens the passenger door and jumps out of the vehicle, breaking her arm as she hits the surface of the road.

Considering the legal concepts regarding an intervening act, which of the comments below is correct?

A CALLAGHAN cannot be held responsible for the actions of RICE which result in her injury as he did not directly inflict them.
B CALLAGHAN can be held liable for the injury caused to RICE if a court considers her actions might reasonably have been anticipated in such a situation.
C CALLAGHAN could only be held liable for the injuries to RICE if he considered that they might take place as a result of his actions.
D CALLAGHAN cannot be held responsible for the injuries caused to RICE as RICE brought them about of her own volition (opening the car door and jumping out of the vehicle).

29. DC FAYED is working in the Criminal Investigation Department at his station when he receives good-quality intelligence from a trusted source in relation to the location of a large amount of stolen goods. The stolen property is alleged to be located at five different premises and, after briefly discussing the matter with his supervisor, DC FAYED decides to make an application to search all the premises (an 'all premises' warrant). Due to the nature of the intelligence received by DC FAYED, he decides to request that the warrant allow entry to the target premises on multiple occasions.

In relation to the procedures under ss. 15 and 16 of the Police and Criminal Evidence Act 1984 (application for a warrant and execution of a warrant) and Code B of the Codes of Practice, which of the following comments is correct?

A Applications for multiple premises and multiple entry warrants must be made with the written authority of an officer of at least the rank of superintendent (although in urgent cases where a superintendent is not readily available, the most senior officer on duty may authorise the application).
B Entry and search under such a warrant must be made within one month from the date of its issue.
C No premises may be entered or searched for the second or any subsequent time under a warrant which authorises multiple entries unless a police officer of at least the rank of inspector has, in writing, authorised that entry to those premises.
D If the warrant is an all premises warrant, no premises which are not specified in it may be entered and searched unless a police officer of at least the rank of superintendent has, in writing, authorised them to be entered.

30. POPESCU, an adult male, has been arrested for several offences of burglary and you intend to search properties that may have evidence relating to the offences that POPESCU has been arrested for. POPESCU occupies a house at 22 Cross Avenue, which he rents from the estate agents Manning and Sons and he also owns and controls a lock-up garage which he uses to keep his car in. You have intelligence at your disposal which indicates that POPESCU rents a storage facility in a warehouse but this is unconfirmed and you only reasonably suspect that he controls the storage facility.

With the correct authorisation from an inspector or above, which of the following statements is correct as to which properties can be searched by a constable under s. 18 of PACE 1984?

A All three properties can be searched.
B The storage facility and the house he rents.
C Only the house he rents.
D The house he rents and his garage.

31. A group of trainee investigators are taking part in an interviewing training course where tactics and techniques in relation to interviewing suspects and witnesses to offences are being discussed. A number of comments are made in relation to the mode of addressing a person being interviewed and the need to avoid language that is demeaning. This generates a discussion in relation to harassment in the workplace and the potential for the Equality Act 2010 to be breached in certain circumstances.

    When considering s. 26 of the Act (in particular, sexual harassment under s. 26(2)), which of the following comments is correct?

    A A man calling another man 'lad' is not demeaning.
    B Referring to women as 'chicks' is not demeaning.
    C Referring to women as 'babes' is not demeaning.
    D Referring to a woman using the term 'sweetie' is not demeaning.

32. BERTRAND attacks CHEUNG in a street and fractures CHEUNG's skull. CHEUNG is rushed to hospital where an examination of CHEUNG shows that the fractured skull has caused brain damage. The seriousness of CHEUNG's situation is compounded by the fact that it is discovered that he has a serious stomach ulcer. The brain damage keeps CHEUNG in a coma and prevents doctors from operating on the stomach ulcer. One month later, the ulcer bursts and causes CHEUNG to die.

    Considering concepts associated with criminal conduct and in particular the 'chain of causation', is BERTRAND liable for the death of CHEUNG?

    A No, because the untreated ulcer, not the fractured skull, was the cause of CHEUNG's death.
    B Yes, CHEUNG's death was a direct consequence of the assault by BERTRAND and, as the chain of causation can never be broken, BERTRAND is liable for CHEUNG's death.
    C No, because of the time delay between the discovery of the ulcer and CHEUNG's death.
    D Yes, but for BERTRAND's attack on CHEUNG, the ulcer could have been operated on and CHEUNG would not have died.

33. SANG has been charged with murder. SANG's defence team have disclosed details of a witness (ASPINALL) they propose to call as an alibi witness for the prosecution and the police officer in charge of the case, Inspector HERON, proposes to conduct an interview with ASPINALL.

    In relation to the Code of Practice for Arranging and Conducting Interviews of Witnesses Notified by the Accused (under s. 21A of the Criminal Procedure and Investigations Act 1996), which of the following comments is correct?

    A ASPINALL is not entitled to be accompanied by a solicitor at the interview.
    B ASPINALL is not obliged to attend the proposed interview.
    C ASPINALL is entitled to be accompanied by a solicitor at the interview; the attendance of the solicitor will be funded by the Legal Services Commission.
    D ASPINALL must be interviewed by an officer of the rank of sergeant or above.

34. HAMPSON has been arrested on suspicion of rape and has been taken to a designated police station. HAMPSON is given his rights by the custody officer, PS CONWAY, and requests that he is represented by MOUAT (his solicitor) whilst he is in police custody. The officer in charge of the case, DC FRANCOMBE, believes that MOUAT will act in a way that will interfere with evidence connected to the rape.

In relation to Code C and HAMPSON's right to legal advice, which of the following comments is correct?

A DC FRANCOMBE should seek a superintendent's authority to deny HAMPSON access to legal advice from MOUAT.
B HAMPSON should be allowed to speak with MOUAT but, to ensure that MOUAT acts ethically, his consultations with HAMPSON can be monitored by a police officer.
C Once the decision has been taken to deny HAMPSON his legal advice, the authorisation applies to all solicitors or legal advisers and lasts up to a maximum of 36 hours.
D HAMPSON cannot be denied access to legal advice from MOUAT in these circumstances.

35. William ABBOTT has been arrested on suspicion of committing an offence of murder. At the time of the offence, Felicity ABBOTT (the wife of William ABBOTT) was with her husband and, although she had no involvement in the offence, she did see exactly what happened. While William ABBOTT is in custody awaiting interview, DC PARRIS (who is part of the investigation team) is gathering evidence and interviews Felicity ABBOTT about the incident. DC PARRIS obtains a witness statement from Felicity ABBOTT describing what she saw occur. William ABBOTT is charged with the murder offence and pleads 'not guilty'.

Considering the law in respect of the compellability of Felicity ABBOTT to give evidence for the prosecution, which of the following statements is correct?

A The statement from Felicity ABBOTT could be admitted in evidence even if she refused to give evidence against her husband.
B Felicity ABBOTT is not compellable to give evidence against her husband in this matter and DC PARRIS should have informed her of this before taking any statement; the statement obtained could not be admitted in evidence.
C Murder is a 'specified offence' under s. 80(2A) of the Police and Criminal Evidence Act 1984, meaning that Felicity ABBOTT is compellable to give evidence for the prosecution.
D A wife cannot be compelled to give evidence against her husband regardless of the crime the husband is accused of.

36. DAVIS is an extremely violent criminal who is part of a gang distributing drugs. DAVIS is arrested for firearms offences and is in police custody at a designated police station and will be interviewed about the offences on video. One of the interviewing officers, DC HAMBLETON, has expert knowledge of the activities of the gang and for that reason the officer in charge of the investigation into the activities of the gang wants DC HAMBLETON to interview DAVIS. DC HAMBLETON tells the officer in charge of the case that he reasonably believes that providing his name during the course of the interview would put him in danger.

Considering the guidance provided by Codes E and F of the Codes of Practice on such matters, which of the following comments is correct?

A The interview should take place as normal but DC HAMBLETON should only provide his warrant number (instead of his name).
B A screen can be provided so that DC HAMBLETON cannot be seen by DAVIS during the course of the interview.
C If an officer of the rank of at least inspector certifies that it is necessary for the officer's safety, DC HAMBLETON should give his warrant number (instead of his name) and also state the police station to which he is attached.
D DC HAMBLETON can take part in the interview but should have his back to the camera and give his warrant number (not his name) and the name of the police station to which he is attached.

37. DODD is the owner of a breakfast/burger van which he pitches in a lay-by on a busy industrial estate. DODD is doing quite well as the quality of his food is good but his success is having an impact on LOWE's similar business which also operates from the industrial estate. LOWE has asked DODD to leave on several occasions and believes he has the right to do so as he was the first to do business on the estate; DODD has ignored him. LOWE is becoming desperate as his business is failing, so he hides an unloaded shotgun beneath his coat and visits DODD's van. DODD is not actually working in the van when LOWE arrives but WEIGHTMAN (DODD's girlfriend) is. LOWE tells WEIGHTMAN that DODD has one week to '*pack up and go*' or there will be consequences. When WEIGHTMAN asks what kind of consequences, LOWE reveals the shotgun and says, '*I will kill your boyfriend*'. LOWE has no intention of following through with his threat but does intend WEIGHTMAN to fear that he will kill DODD. In fact, WEIGHTMAN does not believe LOWE at all.

Considering only the offence of threats to kill (contrary to s. 16 of the Offences Against the Person Act 1861), which of the comments below is true?

A The offence is not committed by DODD as WEIGHTMAN does not believe the threat.
B DODD commits the offence in these circumstances.
C The offence is not committed as the threat was made to a third party (WEIGHTMAN).
D The threat must be made with the intention that the person who receives it will then and there fear for their life or the life of another. As the threat was made to kill DODD in a week's time, LOWE would not commit the offence.

38. BARTON is sitting in the lounge of his house with several friends—they are all watching an international rugby match between England and Scotland. It is a very hot day so he has the windows of the lounge open. During the match, the Scottish team score a try causing BARTON to scream in rage as he is supporting England. He uses extremely abusive language about the Scottish team and, in doing so, he intends to stir up racial hatred against the Scottish. As the windows in the lounge are open, this abusive language is heard by LEISHMAN who is BARTON's neighbour and is Scottish. LEISHMAN contacts the police to complain about BARTON's language. The language was not heard by anyone else.

In relation to the offence under s. 18 of the Public Order Act 1986 (use of words, behaviour or display of written material), which of the following comments is correct?

A The offence has been committed but only in relation to LEISHMAN (as he was not inside the same dwelling as BARTON).
B The offence has not been committed as it cannot be committed by a person who is inside a dwelling.
C The offence has been committed in relation to BARTON's friends in the lounge of his house and also in relation to LEISHMAN.
D The offence is not committed as the language used by BARTON was not heard by anyone except for people in the same dwelling as BARTON or in another dwelling (LEISHMAN).

39. LESTER is in a pub drinking with several friends. THATCHER storms into the pub and approaches LESTER and accuses him of having an affair with his wife (LESTER is a friend of THATCHER's wife but is not having an affair with her). THATCHER shouts that if LESTER does not stop the affair he will tell LESTER's wife and children about the affair and wreck LESTER's life. LESTER tells THATCHER that he is imagining things and that there is no affair taking place. THATCHER shouts *'Right—if you won't admit it, I'll mess your life up and tell your wife and kids now!'* LESTER feels seriously wronged by the accusation and the threat to his family life and loses his temper with THATCHER; he attacks him intending to kill him. Although THATCHER is very badly injured, he survives the attack and LESTER is charged with attempted murder. LESTER states that he lost control when THATCHER threatened to tell his wife and children about a non-existent affair.

Could LESTER use the 'special defence' of loss of control in these circumstances?

A No, as the thing said that caused him to lose control (the 'qualifying trigger') was connected to an accusation of sexual infidelity.
B No, as the loss of control was not related to a fear of serious violence from THATCHER.
C No, as the charge he faces is one of attempted murder and not murder.
D No, as he lost control in relation to a thing threatened to be done rather than a thing done.

40. WHYTE and SCOTT are walking towards JOHNSON'S house. SCOTT's mobile phone rings and SCOTT has a brief conversation and hangs up. SCOTT tells WHYTE that he has to go to his mother's house and cannot accompany WHYTE to JOHNSON's house. SCOTT passes WHYTE a small envelope and asks WHYTE to give it to JOHNSON as JOHNSON is expecting it. WHYTE asks what is in the envelope and SCOTT replies *'£200 cash'*. WHYTE has no reason to disbelieve SCOTT and tells him that he will deliver the money to JOHNSON. WHYTE continues his journey and on the way to JOHNSON's house he is stopped by a police officer. The police officer searches WHYTE and finds the envelope. When the officer opens the envelope, it is found to contain an amount of cocaine and not £200 cash as WHYTE had been informed.

    Is WHYTE in 'possession' of the cocaine?

    A Yes, as he has physical control over it as well as knowledge of its presence.
    B No, as although he knew he had possession of the envelope, he did not know that it contained cocaine.
    C Yes, as all that is required to prove 'possession' is that a person has physical control over something.
    D No, as he thought there was £200 cash inside the envelope.

41. HUTTON and TAGG are standing on a street outside the offices of International Care Ltd and protesting against the activities of the company as they believe the company is involved in animal experiments. HUTTON and TAGG have been speaking to employees of the company as they enter the premises and trying to persuade them not to go into work. PC FITZPATRICK (on uniform patrol) is sent to the incident and, after speaking to HUTTON and TAGG, he forms the opinion that the presence of HUTTON and TAGG at the scene is likely to cause alarm or distress to the employees of International Care Ltd.

    Could PC FITZPATRICK use the powers under s. 42 of the Criminal Justice and Police Act 2001 to direct HUTTON and TAGG to leave the vicinity?

    A No, because a direction to leave the vicinity under s. 42 can only be given by an officer of the rank of inspector or above.
    B Yes, but only because the officer is in uniform.
    C No, because s. 42 powers are only available to prevent the intimidation or harassment of people in their own or others' homes.
    D Yes, and the direction will require HUTTON and TAGG to leave the vicinity and not to return to it within such a period as PC FITZPATRICK may specify, not being for a period longer than three months.

42. PC GOLD (a probationary officer) is the first officer at the scene of a kidnapping offence. Several of his more senior (in terms of experience) colleagues also attend the incident and there is a discussion in relation to the circumstances of the offence. PC GOLD is confused by what his colleagues have said and is unsure of the law relating to the offence of kidnap, so he approaches his supervisor for some advice regarding the offence.

In relation to the offence of kidnap (under common law), which of the comments by officers at the scene of the offence shows a correct understanding of the law?

A PC JOHNSON stated that causing a person to move from place to place when unaccompanied by the defendant would not constitute an offence of kidnap.
B PC ANWAR stated that a person must be taken or carried away by force if the offence is to be committed.
C PC YOUNG stated that if a person is moved only a short distance, the offence will not be made out.
D PC SMETHEM stated that the offence of kidnap cannot be 'attempted'.

43. BROOKER (aged 17 years) is at her parents' home and looking after her child (who is 2 years old). BROOKER is feeling depressed as she feels she has no future career prospects so, to make herself feel a little better about things, she is smoking cannabis (which she does not possess legally). BROOKER smokes a significant amount of cannabis and under the influence of the drug she falls asleep on a settee in the lounge of the house. BROOKER rolls onto her 2-year-old child (who is sleeping next to BROOKER on the settee) and causes the death of her child via suffocation.

In relation to the offence of child cruelty (under s. 1 of the Children and Young Persons Act 1933), which of the following comments is correct?

A The offence has not been committed as the suffocation did not take place when BROOKER was 'in bed' with her child.
B BROOKER can be charged with the offence of child cruelty even though her child has died.
C BROOKER has not committed the offence as she is 17 years old.
D The offence is committed when the person suffocates the child when under the influence of drink; in this situation, BROOKER would not commit the offence.

44. John and Bridget EDMONSON (both 39 years old) are married and live in a house together with Bridget EDMONSON's 60-year-old mother COLOHAN. The relationship between John and Bridget EDMONSON has deteriorated, resulting in John EDMONSON threatening violence towards Bridget EDMONSON on several occasions. COLOHAN has witnessed the threats being made and contacts the police who attend the house during an argument between John and Bridget EDMONSON; the police witness John EDMONSON threatening violence towards Bridget EDMONSON. As a result, the police consider that issuing a Domestic Violence Protection Notice (a DVPN) under s. 24 of the Crime and Security Act 2010 is necessary to protect Bridget EDMONSON.

In relation to the issuing of such a DVPN, which of the following comments is correct?

A If Bridget EDMONSON does not consent to the issuing of a DVPN, then a DVPN cannot be issued.
B The officer authorising the DVPN must consider any representations made by John EDMONSON as to the issuing of a DVPN.
C If a DVPN is issued, then the authorising officer must apply to a magistrates' court for a Domestic Violence Protection Order (a DVPO) no later than 24 hours after the DVPN was issued.
D A DVPN could not require John EDMONSON to leave the house he lives in with Bridget EDMONSON.

45. NEWMAN (a resident of the United Kingdom) goes on a business trip to Turkey. During his trip, he is in a restaurant when he overhears a conversation between two men who are talking about planting a bomb at Heathrow Airport in a month's time. The men state that the bomb will kill hundreds of people and that when it explodes they will claim it as a victory for al-Qaeda against the British government. NEWMAN believes that the information he has heard could help to prevent an act of terrorism. NEWMAN flies home to England two days later but does not say anything to anyone about the conversation he overheard in Turkey.

With regard to the offence of information about acts of terrorism (contrary to s. 38B of the Terrorism Act 2000), which of the following comments is correct?

A NEWMAN must disclose the information as soon as reasonably practicable and this disclosure can be made to any person in authority.
B As NEWMAN was outside the country when he became aware of the information, he could not be charged with this offence if he failed to disclose that information.
C NEWMAN would commit this offence as he believes the information he has might be of material assistance in preventing an act of terrorism.
D NEWMAN has committed this offence to which there is no defence.

46. GLINSKI is planning to carry out a robbery at a post office and decides to use an air rifle during the offence as a means to threaten and frighten staff at the post office into doing as he demands. GLINSKI is convinced that the police are tracking his movements and wants to minimise the risk of his arrest and prosecution so he uses his 14-year-old nephew, PARRY, to take the air rifle to a garage at the rear of the post office and hide it next to several large bins. GLINSKI's plan is to make sure he is not followed to the post office and, once he is happy that that is the case, he will go to the bins, recover the air rifle and commit the robbery.

With regard to the offence of using someone to mind a weapon (contrary to s. 28(1) of the Violent Crime Reduction Act 2006), at what stage, if at all, has an offence first been committed by GLINSKI?

A No offence is committed by GLINSKI as the activity took place with an air weapon and this is not a 'dangerous weapon'.
B No offence is committed by GLINSKI as 'weapons' do not include firearms.
C The offence is first committed when GLINSKI uses PARRY to transport the air rifle to the rear of the post office.
D The offence is first committed when GLINSKI uses PARRY to hide the air rifle next to several large bins.

47. VIVIER is holding a party at his house and has drunk a bottle of gin and is drunk. He decides to set out an obstacle course in his large, private rear garden and challenges his party guests to drive a motorbike (a mechanically propelled vehicle) as fast as they can through the obstacles. Several party guests drive through the course before VIVIER takes his turn. VIVIER is determined to win and accelerates the motorbike to a speed of 50 mph, but as he is going through one of the obstacles a 5-year-old child of one of the party guests runs out in front of him. As VIVIER is drunk, his reactions are slow and he cannot avoid the child and hits the child causing serious head injuries to the child in the process. The child is rushed to hospital but later dies as a result of the serious head injuries.

Could VIVIER be convicted of an offence of causing death by dangerous driving (contrary to s. 1 of the Road Traffic Act 1988) in these circumstances?

A Yes, and the fact that VIVIER was adversely affected by alcohol is, in itself, determinative to prove the offence.
B No, because the death occurred when the child was at a hospital rather than while VIVIER was driving the motorbike.
C Yes, and evidence of drink will be admissible where the quantity of it may have adversely affected the quality of VIVIER's driving.
D No, as the accident took place on private land rather than a road or public place.

48. Police officers visit the home address of INGON and arrest him on suspicion of committing an offence of child abduction (contrary to s. 2 of the Child Abduction Act 1984). Whilst INGON remains on the premises, the officers search his home address and in the process recover a rifle which fires 7.62 mm bullets and an imitation revolver.

In respect of the offence of possessing a firearm while committing or being arrested for a sch. 1 offence (contrary to s. 17(2) of the Firearms Act 1968), which of the following statements is correct?

A INGON commits the offence but this would only be in connection with the rifle.
B The offence is not committed as child abduction is not a sch. 1 offence.
C The offence is committed in respect of the rifle and the imitation firearm.
D INGON can only be found guilty of the s. 17(2) Firearms Act offence if he is found guilty of the child abduction offence first.

49. MALORY hates BRIDGENORTH (her work supervisor). MALORY believes BRIDGENORTH is a petty bureaucrat and picks on her performance with little or no justification, so to get revenge on BRIDGENORTH she posts a letter to his home address. The letter is addressed to BRIDGENORTH's wife and states that BRIDGENORTH has been having an affair with another member of staff and has contracted genital herpes as a result. It is MALORY's intention to cause BRIDGENORTH's wife distress and anxiety when the letter is read. When the letter arrives at BRIDGENORTH's house, BRIDGENORTH's wife opens it and reads it. She is not at all distressed or anxious as she realises this is a blatant lie. She contacts the police regarding the letter.

Does MALORY commit an offence under s. 1(1) of the Malicious Communications Act 1988 (malicious communications)?

A Yes, the offence is completed as soon as the letter is sent.
B No, the letter does not contain a threat.
C Yes, but the offence is not committed until the letter arrives at BRIDGENORTH's house.
D No, as BRIDGENORTH's wife is not caused distress or anxiety.

50. CHALKLEY and McCABE are extremists who are opposed to the activities of a large fast-food chain. The two decide to attack one of the fast-food restaurants and cause damage to the premises. CHALKLEY buys a number of large fireworks which he intends to fire at the restaurants and cause damage; he stores these in the kitchen of his flat. McCABE buys several petrol bombs which she intends to throw at the premises and cause damage; she stores these in a lock-up garage that she rents which is 10 miles from her home.

Would these activities amount to an offence under s. 4 of the Explosives Act 1883 (making or possessing explosives under suspicious circumstances)?

A No, fireworks and petrol bombs are not 'explosive substances' for the purposes of the Explosives Act 1883.
B Yes, but only CHALKLEY would commit the offence in these circumstances.
C No, as the items are going to be used to damage property rather than cause injury to people.
D Yes, CHALKLEY and McCABE would commit the offence in these circumstances.

51. STREET works for a sales company and is considering setting up his own rival business. In order to give his fledgling business a good start, STREET gains unauthorised access to his manager's computer (committing an offence under s. 1 of the Computer Misuse Act 1990 in the process, i.e. 'hacking') intending to write down business-related information contained on his manager's computer screen detailing a large number of influential business contacts.

Is this an offence of unauthorised access with intent to commit further offences (contrary to s. 2 of the Computer Misuse Act 1990)?

A No, because this offence under s. 2 relates to obtaining information for another person to use in the commission of an offence.
B Yes, as STREET has committed an offence of 'unauthorised access' (under s. 1 of the Act) with the relevant intent.
C No, as STREET's activities do not constitute an offence to which this section applies.
D Yes, but STREET must actually obtain and make use of the information before the offence is complete.

52. PC CHARLESWORTH attends the scene of a disturbance where it has been reported that two men are arguing in the street. When the officer arrives, he sees OAKMAN and PRITCHARD shouting at each other. The officer approaches the two men and asks them to calm down, at which point OAKMAN says '*Fuck off, copper!*' and PRITCHARD says '*Mind your own business, pig!*' HALSTEAD (an off-duty police officer) is walking past the incident and, hearing the abuse, walks over to PC CHARLESWORTH, identifies himself and offers to help deal with the situation. Hearing this, OAKMAN punches HALSTEAD in the face (causing a small cut to HALSTEAD's lip) and PRITCHARD kicks PC CHARLESWORTH on the left shin (causing minor bruising). In both cases, the injuries are slight.

Would the Assaults on Emergency Workers (Offences) Act 2019 be relevant to the assaults on PCs CHARLESWORTH and HALSTEAD?

A No, the legislation is not relevant in this situation as it only applies to offences under s. 18 of the Offences Against the Person Act 1861.
B Yes, but only PC CHARLESWORTH would be subject to the legislation.
C No, the legislation is not relevant in this situation as it only applies to offences under ss. 47, 20 and 18 of the Offences Against the Person Act 1861.
D Yes, the legislation would be relevant to PCs CHARLESWORTH and HALSTEAD.

53. DC KINGSTON receives reliable information from a covert human intelligence source (CHIS) that drugs are being stored at a warehouse on a small industrial estate. An operation is commenced in relation to the premises and a warrant (under s. 23 of the Misuse of Drugs Act 1971) is obtained to search the premises and persons within. When the warrant is executed, MILFORD (the owner of the warehouse) is found in an office inside the warehouse in possession of £20,000 worth of cocaine and £50,000 in cash. During the search, the police recover drugs paraphernalia (clingfilm and contact details of drug dealers) from the office. MILFORD is later charged with an offence of possession with intent to supply (contrary to s. 5(3) of the Misuse of Drugs Act 1971).

In relation to proving an intention to supply and potential defences to that offence, which of the following comments is correct?

A Possession of drugs paraphernalia will be evidence that proves the intention to supply.
B In proving an intention to supply, the prosecution would be able to cite as evidence the presence of the £50,000 cash found with the seized drugs.
C MILFORD would be able to utilise the defence under s. 5(4) of the Misuse of Drugs Act 1971 in respect of a charge of possession with intent to supply.
D MILFORD would not be able to utilise the general defence under s. 28 of the Misuse of Drugs Act 1971 Act in respect of a charge of possession with intent to supply.

54. NORRIS is an electrician and visits a Catholic church to carry out some minor repairs on a faulty switch. As NORRIS walks out of the church, LEWIN sees him and presumes NORRIS to be a Catholic. LEWIN intensely dislikes Catholics and decides to damage NORRIS's property because of his hostility towards them. He follows NORRIS to his van and, as NORRIS is opening the van door, LEWIN kicks the van door causing criminal damage to it (contrary to s. 1(1) of the Criminal Damage Act 1971). In fact, NORRIS is a Protestant.

Based on these circumstances alone, has LEWIN committed a religiously aggravated offence?

A Yes, the offence is motivated by religious hostility.
B No, as NORRIS is not a Catholic.
C Yes, all offences under the Criminal Damage Act 1971 can be racially and/or religiously aggravated.
D No, there has been no demonstration of hostility from LEWIN.

55. BERRY is fascinated by Adolf Hitler and the Nazi Party and their treatment and extermination of millions of people in concentration camps in the 1930s and 1940s. He has a collection of Nazi memorabilia on display in the rear living room of his house, including a large swastika flag which has 'Tod der Juden!' ('Death to Jews!') written on it. KAPLAN (who is a Jew) sees the flag and words written on it when he is standing in the rear bedroom of a house that backs on to BERRY's house. KAPLAN is extremely upset at what he sees and contacts the police.

Has BERRY committed an offence under s. 29B of the Public Order Act 1986 (use of words or behaviour or display of written material)?

A Yes, although BERRY would have a defence if he believed the flag on display could not be seen by a person outside his dwelling.
B No, as the written material is displayed by a person inside a dwelling and not seen except by other persons in that or another dwelling.
C Yes, as the flag is threatening and can be seen from outside BERRY's dwelling.
D No, not unless BERRY intends to stir up religious hatred.

56. HEWSON and WHITTACRE are long-term partners and have been living together in the same house for 20 years. HEWSON finds out that WHITTACRE has been having an affair with a work colleague and is fuming about the situation, although she has not confronted WHITTACRE about the affair as she is unsure how to handle the situation. A week after finding out about the affair, WHITTACRE is having a bath at the shared house and HEWSON is in the lounge downstairs drinking whisky. HEWSON has drunk nearly the whole bottle of whisky and is very drunk. She becomes exceptionally angry about WHITTACRE's affair and decides to confront him about it. She goes into the kitchen, grabs a kitchen knife and takes it upstairs and goes into the bathroom. Holding the kitchen knife, HEWSON issues a drunken threat to kill WHITTACRE (there is no one else in the house at this time).

Considering only the offence of affray (contrary to s. 3 of the Public Order Act 1986) and the case law relating to it, which of the following comments is correct?

A The offence of affray is not committed as the activity is taking place in private.
B The offence of affray is not committed as there is only one person (rather than the required two or more persons) threatening unlawful violence.
C The offence of affray has not been committed as HEWSON threatened rather than used violence.
D The offence of affray has not been committed because there is no possibility of a hypothetical bystander fearing for their safety.

57. TURPIN (aged 13 years) has been convicted of an offence of supplying a controlled drug (contrary to s. 4(3) of the Misuse of Drugs Act 1971). The officer in the case is DC FROBISHER who has evidence that suggests that the conviction came about because TURPIN was involved with four other persons who identify themselves as the 'Blue Cap' gang (identifiable by the fact that they wear blue baseball caps) who are heavily involved with drug-related activities. A work colleague suggests to DC FROBISHER that the police could apply for an injunction under s. 34 of the Policing and Crime Act 2009 to prevent TURPIN from engaging in gang-related drug-dealing activity.

Could such an injunction be granted in these circumstances?

A No, as TURPIN is only 13 years old.
B Yes, as long as the court to which the application is made is satisfied beyond all reasonable doubt that TURPIN has engaged in gang-related drug-dealing activity.
C No, as this is not 'gang-related' (a 'gang' consists of five or more people).
D Yes, and if granted the court must attach a power of arrest to any prohibition or requirement in the injunction.

58. BOTHAM has acrimoniously split up with ZAPPE (his long-time girlfriend) and there is a nasty feud between them regarding access to their 6-month-old baby. BOTHAM is chatting to a friend of his on a street corner when he sees ZAPPE walking towards him holding their baby in her arms. Seeing ZAPPE is too much for BOTHAM who loses his temper and runs up to ZAPPE and punches her in the face causing her to lose consciousness for several seconds and fall to the ground causing significant bruising to her face (a more than transient injury). The force of the blow causes ZAPPE to drop the baby and consequently the baby is caused slight injury when it hits the pavement (some minor bruising to the baby's arm).

Thinking about the law relating to offences of assault (particularly the offences of assault contrary to s. 39 of the Criminal Justice Act 1988 and s. 47 of the Offences Against the Person Act 1861), which of the following comments is correct?

A BOTHAM has committed a s. 39 offence against ZAPPE and also the 6-month-old baby (a battery in both cases).
B BOTHAM has committed a s. 39 battery offence against ZAPPE but no offence in relation to the 6-month-old baby.
C BOTHAM has committed a s. 47 assault against ZAPPE and the 6-month-old baby.
D BOTHAM has committed a s. 47 assault against ZAPPE and a s. 39 offence (a battery) against the 6-month-old baby.

59. Kelly SAMUELSON and Amy SAMUELSON are civil partners but have argued and decided to split up. The pair have since argued about who owns what in the house they shared before Kelly moved out three weeks ago. Kelly returns to the house with ORTEGA (her friend) while Amy is at work, with the idea of removing several items of property that Kelly says belong to her. Once inside the house, Kelly becomes upset and says to ORTEGA, *'I don't care about taking my things—smash them instead!'* Kelly and ORTEGA cause damage to a TV in the lounge of the house. The TV belongs to Kelly and also belongs to Amy as they purchased it jointly (a fact that Kelly is aware of). ORTEGA is unaware of this and believes the TV belongs solely to Kelly and that she wants the TV damaged.

Considering the offence of criminal damage (under s. 1(1) of the Criminal Damage Act 1971), which of the following comments is correct?

A ORTEGA would be able to state that she had a 'lawful excuse' to damage the TV if she were charged with criminal damage; Kelly SAMUELSON could be charged with an offence of criminal damage, but such a prosecution could only be instituted with the consent of the DPP.
B ORTEGA has committed criminal damage and has no defence; Kelly SAMUELSON could not be charged with criminal damage as the property belongs to her.
C As the property belongs to Kelly SAMUELSON, no offence of criminal damage has taken place in these circumstances.
D Kelly SAMUELSON and ORTEGA could both be charged with criminal damage; the consent of the DPP is not required as the property damaged also belonged to Amy SAMUELSON.

60. CROFTON knocks on the door of a house owned by WOODWARD. CROFTON tells WOODWARD that he was walking past WOODWARD's house and noticed that the roof was in need of emergency repairs. CROFTON tells WOODWARD that it will not cost much (only £150) and he is in a position to do the work immediately but only if WOODWARD pays him £150 there and then. WOODWARD gives CROFTON £150 and CROFTON promises WOODWARD that he will start the work immediately and states that he will go and get his tools and the equipment to carry out the repairs as he has these in his van which he has parked nearby. CROFTON walks off and does not return; the truth of the matter is that CROFTON never intended to carry out the work.

In relation to the offence of fraud by false representation (contrary to s. 2 of the Fraud Act 2006), which of the following comments is correct?

A The offence has not been committed as the representation that is false must be one as to fact or law—this is a broken promise.
B The offence has been committed as CROFTON's statement (that he will repair the roof) is false—it misrepresents his actual intentions as he never intended to keep the promise he made.
C The offence has been committed although it will be tried summarily as this is low-value fraud (the value of the goods fraudulently obtained does not exceed £200).
D The offence has been committed but would only be complete when WOODWARD gave CROFTON the £150.

61. BARKER is a homeless person who travels from place to place, sleeping in the streets. On a particularly cold night, BARKER becomes concerned that he may die from hypothermia so, purely to obtain shelter from the cold, he breaks into a warehouse office. Once inside the office, he turns on an electric fire to warm himself up. Having warmed up, he decides to look around the office to see if there is anything worth stealing and, after a short search, he finds a jar containing approximately £30 in change which he steals. Curious about the premises he is in, he moves from the warehouse office through a door into a room marked 'Stores'. He walks around the store for several minutes before becoming bored and frustrated at his lot in life and he damages a sink unit in the store. As he is about to leave, he sees a small box containing a number of batteries and, thinking he will be able to sell them, he steals them.

At what stage does BARKER first commit an offence of burglary under s. 9(1)(a) or s. 9(1)(b) of the Theft Act 1968?

A A burglary offence is first committed when BARKER turns on the electric fire.
B A burglary offence is first committed when BARKER steals the £30 in change.
C A burglary offence is first committed when BARKER damages the sink.
D A burglary offence is first committed when BARKER steals the batteries.

62. WILSON funds his lifestyle by committing large-scale credit card fraud. He is arrested using a cloned credit card to purchase goods and taken to a designated police station where a search of his home address (which is 12 miles from the designated police station) is authorised. During the search of WILSON's home address, police officers find 50 blank credit cards and a card-skimming machine. WILSON's computer is seized (from the study of his house) and the credit card data of several hundred people is discovered on the computer. When interviewed, WILSON confesses that he was going to use the blank credit cards, the skimming machine and the data to commit offences of fraud in a few days' time.

In relation to the items found in the search of WILSON's home, does WILSON commit an offence of possession of articles to commit fraud (contrary to s. 6 of the Fraud Act 2006)?

A No, as WILSON did not have the items with him when they were found.
B No, as they were all found in WILSON's home.
C Yes, but only in relation to the 50 blank credit cards and the skimming machine.
D Yes, in relation to the blank credit cards, the skimming machine and the data on his computer.

63. DUBAR has been charged with an offence of handling stolen goods (contrary to s. 22 of the Theft Act 1968). DUBAR has a previous conviction for theft which precedes the date of the handling offence by four years. The police also have evidence that DUBAR had stolen property in his possession from a theft that preceded the handling offence by nine months (he was never charged with an offence relating to that incident).

Which of the following comments is correct in respect of the ability of the prosecution to utilise s. 27 of the Theft Act 1968 (admissibility of previous misconduct for the purpose of proving DUBAR knew or believed the goods to be stolen goods)?

A Provided that seven days' notice in writing is given to DUBAR, the previous conviction is admissible as is the evidence that he was in possession of stolen property nine months ago.
B Provided that seven days' notice in writing is given to DUBAR, the previous conviction is admissible; the evidence that he was in possession of stolen property nine months ago is inadmissible.
C The previous conviction is inadmissible; the evidence that he was in possession of stolen property nine months ago is admissible.
D The previous conviction and the evidence that he was in possession of stolen property nine months ago are both inadmissible.

64. GOLDMAN and CLARKE enter a bank. GOLDMAN approaches a cashier and hands over a note which states, '*Look right—near to the window*'. The cashier looks to his right and, on the other side of the bank, the cashier can see CLARKE (GOLDMAN's accomplice) holding a gun pointing towards the back of an old-age pensioner who is a customer at the bank. The old-age pensioner is completely unaware of the fact that CLARKE has a gun towards his back. GOLDMAN passes another note to the cashier which states, '*Hand over all the money or he gets shot!*' The cashier refuses. GOLDMAN speaks to CLARKE and says '*Do it!*' CLARKE strikes the back of the old-age pensioner's head with the butt of the gun. The customer falls to the ground and CLARKE points the gun at the customer. GOLDMAN looks at the cashier and states, '*Do you think I'm joking? Hand over the money or he gets shot!*' The cashier, fearing for the customer, hands over a large amount of cash.

At what point, if at all, has the offence of robbery been committed?

A When GOLDMAN passes over the first note and the cashier can see the gun being pointed towards the back of the customer.
B When GOLDMAN passes over the second note demanding the money.
C When the cashier hands over a large amount of cash.
D The offence of robbery has not been committed in these circumstances.

65. KOWALSKI is the tenant of house rented from SPRIGG. The rented house has a rear garden which is separated by a small wooden fence from the garden of a house owned by FISHER. On the last day of KOWALSKI's tenancy agreement, she is standing in the back garden of her rented house and looking at some raspberries growing wild in FISHER's rear garden. She decides she will pick and eat some of the raspberries and climbs over the fence into FISHER's garden and picks a dozen raspberries. She climbs back into her rented garden and looks at a dwarf Korean lilac tree that SPRIGG has planted—KOWALSKI has always admired the tree so decides to dig it up and take it with her to her new house.

What is KOWALSKI's liability in relation to the offence of theft (contrary to s. 1(1) of the Theft Act 1968)?

A KOWALSKI is liable for theft but only in relation to the raspberries picked from FISHER's garden.
B KOWALSKI is liable for theft but only in relation to the dwarf Korean lilac tree.
C KOWALSKI is liable for theft in relation to the raspberries picked from FISHER's garden and the dwarf Korean lilac tree.
D KOWALSKI would not commit an offence of theft in these circumstances.

66. DOOLEY breaks into a house owned by LOW with the intention of assaulting LOW and causing him injuries of a s. 47 (Offences Against the Person Act 1861) nature. He forces the front door of LOW's house and walks through the house into the lounge. Whilst in the lounge, he hears a noise upstairs and, believing it to be LOW, he grabs hold of a poker next to the fireplace in the lounge. DOOLEY does not intend to steal the poker but intends to use it on anyone who stands in his way. DOOLEY waits for a few minutes but nothing else happens. He is feeling a little nervous and decides he will keep the poker with him not only to protect himself but also to use it on LOW by smashing it into LOW's skull, thereby fracturing his skull and causing him grievous bodily harm (contrary to s. 18 of the Offences Against the Person Act 1861). DOOLEY moves from the lounge into the hallway of the house with that idea in his mind but then sees blue lights outside the front of the house and realises the police have arrived. He drops the poker in the hallway and runs out of the front door to escape.

Which of the following comments is correct in respect of the offence of burglary?

A DOOLEY commits a burglary (contrary to s. 9(1)(a) of the Theft Act 1968) when he enters the house to carry out a s. 47 assault on LOW.
B DOOLEY commits an aggravated burglary (contrary to s. 10 of the Theft Act 1968) when he picks up the poker.
C DOOLEY commits an aggravated burglary (contrary to s. 10 of the Theft Act 1968) when he enters the hallway of the house with the poker.
D DOOLEY does not commit an offence of burglary in these circumstances.

67. PUGH is owed £200 by CANNON. PUGH has spoken to CANNON about the debt on several occasions but there is no sign of CANNON paying the money back. PUGH has become frustrated by this situation and decides that enough is enough and the next time he sees CANNON he will get his money. He sees CANNON walking along a street and confronts him demanding that the debt be repaid. CANNON becomes annoyed and tells PUGH that he will never repay the money. PUGH produces a knife and holds it to CANNON's face and tells him that unless he pays the debt he will be stabbed. PUGH knows the means he is using to get the debt repaid is wrong but believes that he has a lawful right to have the debt repaid. CANNON refuses, so PUGH cuts CANNON across the face to encourage him to pay up. CANNON panics and hands over £200 from his wallet to PUGH as settlement for the debt. Satisfied that the debt has been settled, PUGH walks away.

At what point, if at all, has the offence of robbery been committed?

A The offence of robbery has not been committed in these circumstances.
B When PUGH produces the knife and holds it to CANNON's face.
C When PUGH uses the knife to cut CANNON across his face.
D When CANNON hands the £200 to PUGH.

72. HANRAHAN and ROE lived together for several years but the relationship ended due to HANRAHAN's violent behaviour. A year after the break up, the pair accidentally meet in a pub. HANRAHAN tells ROE that he is sorry for his past behaviour and is a changed man and wants to get back together with ROE. ROE agrees to this and the pair leave the pub and go to ROE's house where they decide to have sexual intercourse. ROE tells HANRAHAN that she will have sexual intercourse with him on the express condition that he wears a condom during sexual intercourse—HANRAHAN agrees and puts on a condom. As they get into bed together, HANRAHAN removes the condom from his penis (ROE is unaware that HANRAHAN has removed the condom) and has sexual intercourse with ROE without wearing the condom.

Considering the offence of rape (contrary to s. 1 of the Sexual Offences Act 2003), which of the following statements is correct?

A This is not an offence of rape as ROE has consented to the act of sexual intercourse.
B This is an offence of rape (the issue of consent can be determined under s. 74 of the Sexual Offences Act 2003).
C This is not an offence of rape as ROE's consent to sexual intercourse was not obtained by fear or by force.
D This is an offence of rape and the conclusive presumptions in s. 76 of the Sexual Offences Act 2003 would apply to this situation.

73. COMB (a 17-year-old male) approaches NEWTON (a 15-year-old female) in a park and the two chat for 30 minutes, during which time NEWTON tells COMB her age. COMB asks NEWTON if she will meet him at the same location the following day for another chat; NEWTON agrees. The following morning, COMB decides that he will try to touch NEWTON's genitals if he can and walks to the park with that intention; however, he waits at the park in vain as NEWTON has decided not to bother meeting him.

Considering the offence of meeting a child following sexual grooming (contrary to s. 15 of the Sexual Offences Act 2003), which of the following comments is correct?

A The offence is committed when COMB walks to the park as he is travelling to meet NEWTON with the intention of carrying out an offence of sexual activity with a child (contrary to s. 9 of the Sexual Offences Act 2003).
B The offence has not been committed because the communications between the two were not of a sexual nature.
C The offence has not been committed as NEWTON did not meet COMB in the park (on a second occasion).
D The offence has not been committed because COMB is under 18.

74. FITZHARRIS approaches TINNION who is standing alone at a bus stop in the early hours of the morning. FITZHARRIS tells TINNION to stand still, be quiet and let him touch her or he will stab her. TINNION is extremely frightened and does not do anything as FITZHARRIS takes a rolled up newspaper and uses it to touch her breasts through her clothes.

Would this amount to an offence of sexual touching (contrary to s. 3 of the Sexual Offences Act 2003)?

A Yes, and the evidential presumptions under s. 75 of the Sexual Offences Act 2003 would be relevant in the circumstances.
B No, FITZHARRIS did not touch TINNION or anyone else with a part of his body.
C Yes, although the evidential presumptions under s. 75 of the Sexual Offences Act 2003 would not be relevant in the circumstances
D No, because FITZHARRIS touched TINNION through her clothes.

75. BRANNIGAN (aged 17) has accompanied his mother to a care home to visit FROBISHER (a 57-year-old family friend who suffers from cerebral palsy). BRANNIGAN's mother leaves the room FROBISHER lives in to make a phone call, leaving BRANNIGAN in the room with FROBISHER. BRANNIGAN decides that he will sexually assault FROBISHER and intentionally touches her breasts through her clothing—FROBISHER is unable to refuse the sexual touching because of her mental condition and BRANNIGAN is thoroughly aware of this.

Does BRANNIGAN commit an offence of sexual activity with a person with a mental disorder (contrary to s. 30 of the Sexual Offences Act 2003)?

A No, as BRANNIGAN is under 18 years of age.
B Yes, as long as BRANNIGAN touches FROBISHER to obtain sexual gratification.
C No, as the activity does not involve penetration.
D Yes, all the elements of the offence are present.

76. MILBURN (a 47-year-old male) establishes contact with FOSTER (a 15-year-old female) using an internet video communication service. MILBURN lies about his age to FOSTER telling her that he is 15 years old, but he manages to get away with this by telling FOSTER his webcam has a fault and covering it so that he cannot be seen (although he can be heard). During the conversation, MILBURN tells FOSTER how old he is and removes the cover on the webcam so that FOSTER can see him. He then asks FOSTER if she is 'still a virgin' and then begins to masturbate in front of the camera. MILBURN does this to obtain sexual gratification and also intending FOSTER to obtain sexual gratification from watching him masturbate.

Which of the following comments is correct in relation to the offence of engaging in sexual activity in the presence of a child (contrary to s. 11 of the Sexual Offences Act 2003)?

A The offence is committed because MILBURN intends FOSTER to obtain sexual gratification from seeing him masturbate.
B The activity must take place in the physical presence of the child; this has not occurred, so the offence is incomplete.
C MILBURN commits the offence in these circumstances.
D The offence is not committed as FOSTER is 15 years old (it must be in the hearing and/or presence of a child under 13).

77. NELSON is an 18-year-old male and his new girlfriend is LENNON, a 15-year-old female (NELSON is aware of LENNON's age). They have been going out together for a couple of weeks. LENNON is very shy and knows very little about sex. NELSON decides that the only way he is going to be able to have sex with LENNON is to show her pictures of a pornographic nature to lower her inhibitions so that he can achieve sexual gratification at a later date. NELSON at first shows LENNON cartoon still images of persons having sexual intercourse. Then a day later he shows her moving cartoons of persons having sexual intercourse. A week later, as LENNON is now showing more interest, NELSON shows her a pornographic video involving sexual intercourse between males and females via the internet. NELSON believes that after this showing she will have sex with him. LENNON is not amused by this and tells him their relationship is over.

Considering the offence under s. 12 of the Sexual Offences Act 2003 (causing a child to watch a sex act), when if at all does NELSON first commit the offence?

A NELSON does not commit the offence as no sexual gratification was obtained whilst LENNON was exposed to the pornography.
B NELSON commits the offence when he showed her the internet pornography as that was when he believed he would obtain sexual gratification.
C NELSON commits the offence when he shows the moving cartoon pornography.
D NELSON commits the offence when he shows LENNON the first pornographic cartoon still image.

78. CHENG was attacked by WALKER who attempted to subject CHENG to a sexual assault which would have amounted to an offence under s. 2 of the Sexual Offences Act 2003 (assault by penetration). CHENG fought WALKER off and WALKER was later arrested and charged with an attempt to commit assault by penetration (under the Criminal Attempts Act 1981). CHENG is extremely concerned about her identity becoming known and the stigma she feels this will bring to her in the local community. She approaches the officer in the case, DC ALDENKAMP, for some advice regarding anonymity.

In relation to anonymity and the provisions of s. 1 of the Sexual Offences (Amendment) Act 1992, which of the following statements is correct?

A CHENG would not be entitled to anonymity under the Act as this only applies to victims of an offence of rape (contrary to s. 1 of the Sexual Offences Act 2003).
B CHENG would be entitled to anonymity throughout her lifetime and this would be the case even if proceedings against WALKER were later abandoned.
C CHENG would be entitled to anonymity for a period of 20 years beginning with the date that WALKER is accused of the offence.
D CHENG would not be entitled to anonymity under the Act as WALKER has not been charged with an offence under the Sexual Offences Act 2003—he has been charged with an attempt to commit such an act.

79. WESCOTT is at a house party and has been drinking so heavily that she has fallen unconscious. Her friends take her to a bedroom in the house and leave her in a bed to sleep for the rest of the night. ALLSOPP and GREY have seen what has happened and go into the bedroom where WESCOTT is sleeping and remove WESCOTT's clothing. ALLSOPP takes hold of WESCOTT's hand and places one of her fingers in his anus while GREY puts his penis in WESCOTT's mouth.

Considering only the offence of assault by penetration (contrary to s. 2 of the Sexual Offences Act 2003), which of the comments below is correct?

A The offence has not been committed in these circumstances.
B ALLSOPP has committed the offence, GREY has not.
C GREY has committed the offence, ALLSOPP has not.
D ALLSOPP and GREY have committed the offence.

80. MILLER and CAVANAH have been going out together for several weeks. MILLER has suggested sexual intercourse to CAVANAH but she has politely refused him; this has annoyed MILLER. The pair pay a visit a restaurant for a meal and during the meal MILLER sees a member of staff (GREENFIELD) serving drinks at the restaurant bar. MILLER knows GREENFIELD very well and approaches him and offers him £200 to put large amounts of alcohol in the cocktails that CAVANAH is drinking (CAVANAH does not drink alcohol and is drinking non-alcoholic cocktails). MILLER's intention is to get CAVANAH drunk so that he can have sexual intercourse with her. GREENFIELD asks MILLER why he wants him to put alcohol in CAVANAH's drink and, when MILLER tells him, he thinks it is funny and agrees to do as MILLER requests. Over a period of three hours, CAVANAH becomes very drunk and is violently sick, so much so that the staff at the restaurant call for an ambulance and she is taken to hospital; meaning that MILLER does not have the opportunity to have sexual intercourse with her.

In relation to the offence of administering a substance with intent (contrary to s. 61 of the Sexual Offences Act 2003), which of the following statements is correct?

A 'Spiking' CAVANAH's soft drink with alcohol would not amount to an offence under s. 2 of the Act (alcohol is not a 'substance').
B GREENFIELD does not commit the offence as the alcohol was introduced to CAVANAH's non-alcoholic drink so that MILLER (rather than GREENFIELD) could engage in sexual activity with CAVANAH.
C MILLER and GREENFIELD would commit the offence in this situation.
D Only GREENFIELD would commit the offence in this situation.

OXFORD
UNIVERSITY PRESS

Blackstone's Police Investigators' Mock Examination Paper 2024

Answer Sheet

1 ⊏A⊐ ⊏B⊐ ⊏C⊐ ⊏D⊐
2 ⊏A⊐ ⊏B⊐ ⊏C⊐ ⊏D⊐
3 ⊏A⊐ ⊏B⊐ ⊏C⊐ ⊏D⊐
4 ⊏A⊐ ⊏B⊐ ⊏C⊐ ⊏D⊐
5 ⊏A⊐ ⊏B⊐ ⊏C⊐ ⊏D⊐

6 ⊏A⊐ ⊏B⊐ ⊏C⊐ ⊏D⊐
7 ⊏A⊐ ⊏B⊐ ⊏C⊐ ⊏D⊐
8 ⊏A⊐ ⊏B⊐ ⊏C⊐ ⊏D⊐
9 ⊏A⊐ ⊏B⊐ ⊏C⊐ ⊏D⊐
10 ⊏A⊐ ⊏B⊐ ⊏C⊐ ⊏D⊐

11 ⊏A⊐ ⊏B⊐ ⊏C⊐ ⊏D⊐
12 ⊏A⊐ ⊏B⊐ ⊏C⊐ ⊏D⊐
13 ⊏A⊐ ⊏B⊐ ⊏C⊐ ⊏D⊐
14 ⊏A⊐ ⊏B⊐ ⊏C⊐ ⊏D⊐
15 ⊏A⊐ ⊏B⊐ ⊏C⊐ ⊏D⊐

16 ⊏A⊐ ⊏B⊐ ⊏C⊐ ⊏D⊐
17 ⊏A⊐ ⊏B⊐ ⊏C⊐ ⊏D⊐
18 ⊏A⊐ ⊏B⊐ ⊏C⊐ ⊏D⊐
19 ⊏A⊐ ⊏B⊐ ⊏C⊐ ⊏D⊐
20 ⊏A⊐ ⊏B⊐ ⊏C⊐ ⊏D⊐

21 ⊏A⊐ ⊏B⊐ ⊏C⊐ ⊏D⊐
22 ⊏A⊐ ⊏B⊐ ⊏C⊐ ⊏D⊐
23 ⊏A⊐ ⊏B⊐ ⊏C⊐ ⊏D⊐
24 ⊏A⊐ ⊏B⊐ ⊏C⊐ ⊏D⊐
25 ⊏A⊐ ⊏B⊐ ⊏C⊐ ⊏D⊐

26 ⊏A⊐ ⊏B⊐ ⊏C⊐ ⊏D⊐
27 ⊏A⊐ ⊏B⊐ ⊏C⊐ ⊏D⊐
28 ⊏A⊐ ⊏B⊐ ⊏C⊐ ⊏D⊐
29 ⊏A⊐ ⊏B⊐ ⊏C⊐ ⊏D⊐
30 ⊏A⊐ ⊏B⊐ ⊏C⊐ ⊏D⊐

31 ⊏A⊐ ⊏B⊐ ⊏C⊐ ⊏D⊐
32 ⊏A⊐ ⊏B⊐ ⊏C⊐ ⊏D⊐
33 ⊏A⊐ ⊏B⊐ ⊏C⊐ ⊏D⊐
34 ⊏A⊐ ⊏B⊐ ⊏C⊐ ⊏D⊐
35 ⊏A⊐ ⊏B⊐ ⊏C⊐ ⊏D⊐

36 ⊏A⊐ ⊏B⊐ ⊏C⊐ ⊏D⊐
37 ⊏A⊐ ⊏B⊐ ⊏C⊐ ⊏D⊐
38 ⊏A⊐ ⊏B⊐ ⊏C⊐ ⊏D⊐
39 ⊏A⊐ ⊏B⊐ ⊏C⊐ ⊏D⊐
40 ⊏A⊐ ⊏B⊐ ⊏C⊐ ⊏D⊐

41 ⊏A⊐ ⊏B⊐ ⊏C⊐ ⊏D⊐
42 ⊏A⊐ ⊏B⊐ ⊏C⊐ ⊏D⊐
43 ⊏A⊐ ⊏B⊐ ⊏C⊐ ⊏D⊐
44 ⊏A⊐ ⊏B⊐ ⊏C⊐ ⊏D⊐
45 ⊏A⊐ ⊏B⊐ ⊏C⊐ ⊏D⊐

46 ⊏A⊐ ⊏B⊐ ⊏C⊐ ⊏D⊐
47 ⊏A⊐ ⊏B⊐ ⊏C⊐ ⊏D⊐
48 ⊏A⊐ ⊏B⊐ ⊏C⊐ ⊏D⊐
49 ⊏A⊐ ⊏B⊐ ⊏C⊐ ⊏D⊐
50 ⊏A⊐ ⊏B⊐ ⊏C⊐ ⊏D⊐

51 ⊏A⊐ ⊏B⊐ ⊏C⊐ ⊏D⊐
52 ⊏A⊐ ⊏B⊐ ⊏C⊐ ⊏D⊐
53 ⊏A⊐ ⊏B⊐ ⊏C⊐ ⊏D⊐
54 ⊏A⊐ ⊏B⊐ ⊏C⊐ ⊏D⊐
55 ⊏A⊐ ⊏B⊐ ⊏C⊐ ⊏D⊐

56 ⊏A⊐ ⊏B⊐ ⊏C⊐ ⊏D⊐
57 ⊏A⊐ ⊏B⊐ ⊏C⊐ ⊏D⊐
58 ⊏A⊐ ⊏B⊐ ⊏C⊐ ⊏D⊐
59 ⊏A⊐ ⊏B⊐ ⊏C⊐ ⊏D⊐
60 ⊏A⊐ ⊏B⊐ ⊏C⊐ ⊏D⊐

61 ⊏A⊐ ⊏B⊐ ⊏C⊐ ⊏D⊐
62 ⊏A⊐ ⊏B⊐ ⊏C⊐ ⊏D⊐
63 ⊏A⊐ ⊏B⊐ ⊏C⊐ ⊏D⊐
64 ⊏A⊐ ⊏B⊐ ⊏C⊐ ⊏D⊐
65 ⊏A⊐ ⊏B⊐ ⊏C⊐ ⊏D⊐

66 ⊏A⊐ ⊏B⊐ ⊏C⊐ ⊏D⊐
67 ⊏A⊐ ⊏B⊐ ⊏C⊐ ⊏D⊐
68 ⊏A⊐ ⊏B⊐ ⊏C⊐ ⊏D⊐
69 ⊏A⊐ ⊏B⊐ ⊏C⊐ ⊏D⊐
70 ⊏A⊐ ⊏B⊐ ⊏C⊐ ⊏D⊐

71 ⊏A⊐ ⊏B⊐ ⊏C⊐ ⊏D⊐
72 ⊏A⊐ ⊏B⊐ ⊏C⊐ ⊏D⊐
73 ⊏A⊐ ⊏B⊐ ⊏C⊐ ⊏D⊐
74 ⊏A⊐ ⊏B⊐ ⊏C⊐ ⊏D⊐
75 ⊏A⊐ ⊏B⊐ ⊏C⊐ ⊏D⊐

76 ⊏A⊐ ⊏B⊐ ⊏C⊐ ⊏D⊐
77 ⊏A⊐ ⊏B⊐ ⊏C⊐ ⊏D⊐
78 ⊏A⊐ ⊏B⊐ ⊏C⊐ ⊏D⊐
79 ⊏A⊐ ⊏B⊐ ⊏C⊐ ⊏D⊐
80 ⊏A⊐ ⊏B⊐ ⊏C⊐ ⊏D⊐

Marking instructions

- Mark like this ~~A~~
- Make no stray marks
- Please do **NOT** tick, cross or circle

OXFORD
UNIVERSITY PRESS

Blackstone's Police Investigators' Mock Examination Paper 2024

Pack 2

Contents

DO NOT OPEN THIS ANSWER PACK UNTIL YOU HAVE COMPLETED THE MOCK EXAM

OXFORD UNIVERSITY PRESS	Blackstone's Police Investigators' Mock Examination Paper 2024

Marking Instructions

Lay your answer sheet next to the marking matrix and begin the marking process. Starting with Question 1, compare your marked answer with the correct answer given in the marking matrix. If the correct answer matches your marked answer, put a '✓' mark inside the white box on the relevant row (see questions 1, 2 and 4 below). If it does not (see Question 3) put an 'X' mark.

Question	Answer	General Principles, Police Powers and Procedures	Random Non-counting MCQ
1	D	✓	
2	C	✓	
3	A	✗	
4	C		✓

The first 36 questions in the Mock Examination all relate to Part 1 of the syllabus, 'General Principles, Police Powers and Procedures' however, you will see that not all of the 36 questions will count towards your mark as 6 questions within this block of 36 have been designated as a 'Random Non-counting MCQ'. This is in order to reflect the nature of the marking process used in your NIE.

When you have marked the first 36 questions, add up the total for the 'General Principles, Police Powers and Procedures' column to give you a mark out of 30.

35	A	✓	
36	D	✗	
Total	=	18/30	

Then do the same for Questions 37 to 58 ('Serious Crime and Other Offences'), Questions 59 to 68 ('Property Offences') and Questions 69 to 80 ('Sexual Offences').

Enter the totals for each block of questions in the 'Final Score' table and add them up to reach a final total (out of 70) for the whole exam.

Compare your final score to the table underneath the 'Final Score', which will indicate whether or not you have passed the mock examination. The pass mark for the exam is 39.

Marking Matrix, Questions 1–36

Question	Answer	General Principles, Police Powers and Procedures	Random Non-counting MCQ
1	D		
2	C		
3	A		
4	C		
5	C		
6	D		
7	B		
8	A		
9	B		
10	A		
11	C		
12	B		
13	B		
14	A		
15	C		
16	D		
17	C		
18	D		
19	B		
20	A		
21	A		
22	A		
23	C		
24	B		
25	A		
26	C		
27	B		
28	B		
29	C		
30	D		
31	A		
32	D		
33	B		
34	A		
35	A		
36	D		
Total	=	/30	

Marking Matrix, Questions 37–58

Question	Answer	Serious Crime and Other Offences	Random Non-counting MCQ
37	B		
38	D		
39	C		
40	A		
41	C		
42	A		
43	B		
44	B		
45	C		
46	A		
47	D		
48	C		
49	A		
50	D		
51	C		
52	D		
53	B		
54	A		
55	B		
56	D		
57	A		
58	D		
Total	=	/20	

Marking Matrix, Questions 59–68

Question	Answer	Property Offences	Random Non-counting MCQ
59	A		
60	B		
61	B		
62	D		
63	A		
64	C		
65	D		
66	C		
67	A		
68	A		
Total	=	/9	

Marking Matrix, Questions 69–80

Question	Answer	Sexual Offences	Random Non-counting MCQ
69	B		
70	A		
71	A		
72	B		
73	D		
74	A		
75	D		
76	C		
77	D		
78	B		
79	C		
80	C		
Total	=	/11	

Final Score

Syllabus Area	*Marks*
General Principles etc.	**/30**
Serious Crime and Other Offences	**/20**
Property Offences	**/9**
Sexual Offences	**/11**
TOTAL =	**/70**

Questions right	% score	Questions right	% score	Questions right	% score	Questions right	% score	Questions right	% score
1	1.429	15	21.429	29	41.429	43	61.429	57	81.429
2	2.857	16	22.857	30	42.857	44	62.857	58	82.857
3	4.286	17	24.286	31	44.286	45	64.286	59	84.286
4	5.714	18	25.714	32	45.714	46	65.714	60	85.714
5	7.143	19	27.143	33	47.143	47	67.143	61	87.143
6	8.571	20	28.571	34	48.571	48	68.571	62	88.571
7	10	21	30	35	50	49	70	63	90
8	11.429	22	31.429	36	51.429	50	71.429	64	91.429
9	12.857	23	32.857	37	52.857	51	72.857	65	92.857
10	14.286	24	34.286	38	54.286	52	74.286	66	94.286
11	15.714	25	35.714	39	55.714	53	75.714	67	95.714
12	17.143	26	37.143	40	57.143	54	77.143	68	97.143
13	18.571	27	38.571	41	58.571	55	78.571	69	98.571
14	20	28	40	42	60	56	80	70	100

OXFORD
UNIVERSITY PRESS

Blackstone's Police Investigators' Mock Examination Paper 2024

Answer Booklet

1. Answer **D** — A non-intimate sample may be taken from a detainee in a variety of circumstances (see para. 6.6 of Code D). This applies whether or not the person is a juvenile, making answer A incorrect. Code D, para. 6.7 states that reasonable force may be used, if necessary, to take a non-intimate sample from a person without their consent and does not require the authority of an inspector or above, making answer B incorrect. Code D, para. 6.10 states that a record will be made of the process and, if force is used, the record will include the circumstances and those present. Written consent does not have to be provided by the detainee, making answer C incorrect.

Investigators' Manual, para. 1.8.7.4

2. Answer **C** — The Magistrates' Courts Rules 1981, r. 99, as amended by the Magistrates' Courts (Amendment) Rules 2019 (SI 2019/1367), states:

(1) Subject to paragraph (7), a summons requiring a person to appear before a magistrates' court may be served by—
(a) handing it to the person in person or, where the person is a corporation, to a person holding a senior position in that corporation;
(b) posting it to the person at an address where it is reasonably believed that the person will receive it or, where the person is a corporation, the address for service in accordance with paragraph (2);
(c) addressing it to the person and leaving it for the person at an address where it is reasonably believed that the person will receive it;
(d) where the person has given an electronic address and has not refused to accept service at that address, sending it by electronic means to the address which the person has given;
(e) where the person to be served is given access to an electronic address at which a document may be deposited and has not refused to accept service by the deposit of a document at that address, by depositing it at that address and making it possible for the recipient to read the document, or view or listen to its content, as the case may be, and notifying the recipient of the deposit of the document (which notice may be given by electronic means);
(f) where the person is in custody, sending it to his or her custodian, addressed to the person;
(g) where the person has given a document exchange (DX) box number, and has not refused to accept service by DX, addressing it to the person at that DX box number and leaving it at that document exchange;

(h) where the person is legally represented, serving it on the person's legal representative in the same manner as it could be served on the person under subparagraphs (a), (b), (c) and (g);
(i) where the person is legally represented and the person's legal representative has given an electronic address, sending it to that address;
(j) where the person to be served is legally represented and the legal representative is given access to an electronic address at which a document may be deposited by depositing it at that address and making it possible for the recipient to read the document, or view or listen to its content, as the case may be, and notifying the recipient of the deposit of the document (which notice may be given by electronic means); or
(k) any other method specified by the court.

Answer A is incorrect as the documents can be served on RANKINE's legal representative. Answer B is incorrect as the documents can be served on RANKINE. Answer D is incorrect as the documents can be served electronically. The documents can be served on RANKINE or FINLEY (correct answer C).

Investigators' Manual, para. 1.4.3

3. Answer **A** — The Youth Justice and Criminal Evidence Act 1999 provides that both prosecution and defence witnesses are eligible for special measures, and the categories of eligibility include:

- all witnesses under the age of 18 at the time of the hearing or video recording (s. 16(1)(a));
- vulnerable witnesses who are affected by a mental disorder, impairment of intelligence and social functioning (s. 16(2)(a)(i), (ii));
- vulnerable witnesses who are affected by physical disability or disorder (s. 16(2)(b));
- witnesses in fear or distress about testifying (s. 17(1));
- any witness to a 'relevant offence', currently defined to include homicide offences and other offences involving a firearm or knife (s. 17(5)–(7), sch. 1A);
- adult victims of domestic violence who are vulnerable or intimidated;
- adult complainants of sexual offences (as defined by s. 62 of the 1999 Act), human trafficking offences (s. 59A of the Sexual Offences Act 2003 or s. 4 of the Asylum and Immigration (Treatment of Claimants, etc.) Act 2004), indecent photographs of children offences (s. 1 of the Protection of Children Act 1978 (take, permit to be taken or publish etc. such a photograph), s. 160 of the Criminal Justice Act 1988 (possession of such a photograph)), slavery and trafficking offences (ss. 1 and 2 of the Modern Slavery Act 2015) and an offence of domestic abuse under the Domestic Abuse Act 2021.

The eligibility criteria means that answer D is incorrect. In relation to the category 'any witness to a "relevant offence" involving a firearm, offensive weapon or knife', the 'relevant offence' is an offence specified in sch. 1A to the 1999 Act that includes murder, manslaughter, wounding, assault etc. All witnesses involved in such cases, including police officers, are automatically eligible for a special measures direction unless they decline (s. 17(5)), this means that answer B is incorrect. Answer C is incorrect as the primary rule is that all witnesses under the age of 18, regardless of the nature of the offence charged, are eligible for their evidence to be given by video interview and the use of live link; this does not prohibit a child witness who wishes to testify in court (ss. 21 and 22) (correct answer A).

Investigators' Manual, para. 1.5.9.1

4. Answer **C** — Powers to enter under s. 17 are available to officers for many reasons. Pursuing a person who is unlawfully at large and whom the officer is pursuing is one of those reasons (s. 17(1)(d)) as is the power to enter, search and arrest for an indictable offence (s. 17(1)(b))—but these are not the only reasons an officer may enter under s. 17, meaning that answers B and D are incorrect. The Police and Criminal Evidence Act 1984, s. 17(1)(c)(iii) states that a constable may enter and search any premises for the purpose of arresting a person for an offence under s. 4 of the Public Order Act 1986 (fear or provocation of violence). The officer does not have to be in uniform to exercise the power under s. 17(1)(c)(iii), making answer A incorrect. Force may be used if necessary, meaning that answer C is correct.

Investigators' Manual, para. 1.6.7

5. Answer **C** — Special safeguards apply in relation to the authorisation of juveniles and vulnerable individuals as 'CHIS'. Juveniles are those under 18 years of age. On no occasion should the use or conduct of a CHIS under 16 years of age be authorised to give information against their parents or any person who has parental responsibility for them (but this would not stop OTTER providing information about his uncle, making answer D incorrect). Answer B is incorrect as although a person under 16 cannot be used as a CHIS to provide information about their parents or a person with parental responsibility for them, this does not stop those under 16 being a CHIS (albeit that authorisations should not be granted unless the special provisions contained within the Regulation of Investigatory Powers (Juveniles) (Amendment) Order 2018 (SI 2018/715) are satisfied).

   A CHIS authorisation for a juvenile/vulnerable CHIS lasts four months beginning on the day authorisation is granted (making answer A incorrect).

Investigators' Manual, para. 1.12.3

6. Answer **D** — An eyewitness may be taken to a particular neighbourhood or place to see whether they can identify the person they saw. It is not necessary for the eyewitness to be accompanied by two officers, making answer C incorrect. Where it is practicable, a record should be made of the eyewitness's description of the suspect before asking the eyewitness to make an identification in such a manner, so rather than being a bar to taking part in a 'street' identification, the first description is a desirable element, making answer A incorrect. Care must be taken not to provide the eyewitness with any information concerning the description of the suspect (if such information is available) and not to direct the eyewitness's attention to any individual unless, taking into account all the circumstances, this cannot be avoided. However, this does not prevent an eyewitness being asked to look carefully at the people standing around at the time or to look towards a group or in a particular direction, if this is necessary to make sure the eyewitness does not overlook a possible suspect simply because they are looking in the opposite direction, making answer B incorrect. Answer D is correct as the officer has complied with the Codes of Practice (Code D, para. 3.2).

Investigators' Manual, paras 1.8.4 to 1.8.4.2

7. Answer **B** — PACE s. 55A allows a person who has been arrested and is in police detention to have an X-ray taken of them or an ultrasound scan to be carried out on them (or both) if:

   (a) authorised by an officer of the rank of inspector or above who has reasonable grounds for believing that the detainee:
      (i) may have swallowed a Class A drug; and
      (ii) was in possession of that Class A drug with the intention of supplying it to another or to export; and
   (b) the detainee's appropriate consent has been given in writing.

   No force can be used, making B the correct answer.

   Investigators' Manual, para. 1.7.27

8. Answer **A** — The right under s. 56 of the Police and Criminal Evidence Act 1984 may be delayed if authorised by an officer of the rank of inspector or above (making answers C and D incorrect). The maximum period that the right can be delayed is 36 hours (making answer B incorrect).

   Investigators' Manual, para. 1.7.23

9. Answer **B** — Code C, para. 12.2 states that except as below, in any period of 24 hours a detainee must be allowed a continuous period of at least eight hours for rest, free from questioning, travel or any interruption in connection with the investigation concerned. This period should normally be at night or other appropriate time which takes account of when the detainee last slept or rested. If a detainee is arrested at a police station after going there voluntarily, the period of 24 hours runs from the time of their arrest and not the time of arrival at the police station, making answer C incorrect. The period may not be interrupted or delayed, except:

   (a) when there are reasonable grounds for believing not delaying or interrupting the period would:
      (i) involve a risk of harm to people or serious loss of, or damage to, property;
      (ii) delay unnecessarily the person's release from custody; or
      (iii) otherwise prejudice the outcome of the investigation;
   (b) at the request of the detainee, their appropriate adult or legal representative;
   (c) when a delay or interruption is necessary in order to:
      (i) comply with the legal obligations and duties arising under section 15; or
      (ii) to take action required under *section 9* or in accordance with medical advice.

   So answer D is incorrect as while para. 12.2(a)(i) is *one* of the reasons the rest period can be interrupted, it is one of many. Answer A is incorrect as para. 12.2(b) states that the rest period can be legitimately interrupted at the request of a legal representative. If the period is interrupted in accordance with sub-para. (a), a fresh period must be allowed. Interruptions under sub-paras (b) and (c) do not require a fresh period to be allowed (correct answer B).

   Investigators' Manual, para. 1.9.4

10. Answer **A** — Whether or not a defendant is legally represented in an interview will not prevent adverse inferences being drawn (unless the defendant is being held incommunicado and legal advice has been withheld after the defendant has requested a solicitor), making answer D

incorrect. A defendant cannot be convicted solely on an adverse inference drawn from silence, making answer B incorrect. Adverse inferences can be drawn from an interview where the suspect remains silent, responds 'no comment' to questioning or fails to mention any fact relied on in their defence in proceedings, making answer C incorrect.

Investigators' Manual, para. 1.9.2.3

11. Answer **C** — A joint criminal enterprise exists where two (or more) people embark on the commission of an offence by one or both (or all) of them. It is a joint enterprise because all the parties have a common goal—that an offence will be committed. In this case, there is a 'joint enterprise' as GUNNEL and PLEYDEN have agreed to steal a car from a garage (an offence of burglary). As the parties to a joint enterprise share a combined purpose, each would be liable for the consequences of the actions of the other in the pursuit of their joint enterprise. This would indicate that GUNNEL is liable for the injury to HENDERSON but that is not the case (answers A and B are incorrect). Where the actions of one party to the joint enterprise are a departure from what was agreed, what is described as 'parasitic accessory liability' (where GUNNEL would be liable for the injury to HENDERSON) will not apply (correct answer C). A good example is provided by the *Crime Manual* where two men (A and B) agree to carry out an offence of theft. During the course of the offence, the owner of the property subject of the offence appears and tries to prevent the offence taking place. Offender A produces a flick-knife and stabs the victim, causing grievous bodily harm. Offender B had no idea that offender A had a flick-knife and had never contemplated the use of violence during the theft offence. The actions of offender A are a departure from the nature and type of crime that was envisaged by offender B who did not know that A possessed a flick-knife; it is an act so fundamentally different from that originally contemplated by B, that B is most unlikely to be liable for the injuries caused to the victim (*R* v *Anderson* [1966] 2 QB 110)—you can see how this example connects to the scenario in the MCQ. Answer D is incorrect as an accessory does not have to physically take part in an offence to be liable for it.

Investigators' Manual, paras 1.3.8 to 1.3.8.2

12. Answer **B** — If a juvenile's parent is estranged from the juvenile, he/she should not be asked to act as the appropriate adult if the juvenile expressly and specifically objects to their presence (see Keynote to Code C 1.7), making answers A, C and D incorrect.

Investigators' Manual, para. 1.7.6

13. Answer **B** — A constable may require a person to attend a police station for the purpose of taking his/her fingerprints under s. 61(5A) when they have been arrested for a recordable offence and released, and the fingerprints that were taken were of insufficient quality (answer D is incorrect). If a person fails to comply with the requirement, that person can be arrested without warrant (answer A is incorrect). The person must be given a period of at least seven days within which to attend the police station (answer C is incorrect). If there is an urgent need for MASON's fingerprints to be obtained for the purposes of the investigation of the offence, an officer of the rank of inspector or above may authorise a period shorter than seven days for MASON to attend the police station (Annex G, para. 3—correct answer B).

Investigators' Manual, para. 1.8.14

14. Answer **A** — Section 25 of the Criminal Justice and Public Order Act 1994 applies when a defendant is charged with murder, attempted murder, manslaughter and a host of offences under the Sexual Offences Act 2003 and has a conviction for one of those offences. This makes answer D incorrect. There are no time limitations relating to when the previous conviction was obtained, making answer B incorrect. A defendant charged with one of the above offences, and with a previous conviction for one of the above offences, will not be granted bail unless there are exceptional circumstances which justify it, making answer C incorrect.

Investigators' Manual, para. 1.10.5

15. Answer **C** — Answer A is incorrect as Professional Standards Departments (PSDs) have final responsibility for the value judgement on whether information relating to misconduct of police officers should be revealed to the prosecutor. Answer D is incorrect as not only might the credibility of witnesses undermine the prosecution case, but so too might complaints against officers involved in the case, together with any occasions where officers have not been believed in court in the past. In these cases, it will be necessary to decide whether this information should be disclosed to the defence and, if disclosed, in how much detail. Advice given to prosecutors can assist when considering complaints and misconduct of police officers. The advice states:

    It is, of course, necessary in the first instance for the police to bring such matters to the notice of the prosecutor, but it is submitted that the prosecutor should have a greater element of discretion than with the disclosure of previous convictions. With convictions against prosecution witnesses, disclosure normally follows, whereas in relation to disciplinary findings regard should be had to the nature of the finding and its likely relevance to the matters in issue. Findings which involve some element of dishonesty should invariably be disclosed, while matters such as disobedience to orders, neglect of duty and discreditable conduct will often have no relevance to the officer's veracity or the guilt or otherwise of a defendant. Certainly, there should be no duty on the prosecution to disclose details of unsubstantiated complaints even though this is a popular type of inquiry from some defence representatives. The imposition of such a duty would only encourage the making of false complaints in the hope that they might be used to discredit an officer in the future.

    There is no absolute requirement to disclose findings in relation to disciplinary matters (answer B is incorrect). Answer C is correct as per the above passage of text.

Investigators' Manual, para. 1.11.6.5

16. Answer **D** — Section 54A of the Police and Criminal Evidence Act 1984 (as inserted by the Anti-terrorism, Crime and Security Act 2001) provides a power to search and/or examine detained persons without their consent. This must be in order to ascertain whether the person has any mark that would tend to identify him/her as a person involved in the commission of an offence or to assist to identify him/her. Mark includes features and injuries. The search/examination is authorised by an officer of at least the rank of inspector. Authorisation may be given orally or in writing but if given orally it must be confirmed in writing as soon as possible.

Investigators' Manual, paras 1.8.6 to 1.8.6.1

17. Answer **C** — There is no specific provision within the Police and Criminal Evidence Act 1984 or the Codes of Practice for the disclosure of any information by the police at the police station,

with the exception of the custody record (so the custody record must be disclosed, making answers A and B incorrect). In respect of the provision of a copy of the 'first description' of a suspect, it should be noted that Code D (para. 3.1) states that a copy of the 'first description' shall, where practicable, be given to the suspect or his/her solicitor before any procedures under paras 3.5 to 3.10, 3.21 or 3.23 are carried out. In other words, the disclosure requirement is that a copy of the 'first description' shall, where practicable, be given to the suspect or his/her solicitor before a video identification, an identification parade, a group identification or confrontation takes place. Therefore, an officer disclosing information to a solicitor at the interview stage (which is taking place in advance of any identification procedures) need not provide the 'first description' of a suspect at that time.

Further, there is nothing within the Criminal Justice and Public Order Act 1994 that states that information must be disclosed before an inference from silence can be made (making answer D incorrect).

Investigators' Manual, para. 1.9.4.3

18. Answer **D** — There are a number of reasons that an interview may be recorded in writing. Code E, para. 2.3 states that a written record of the matters described in para. 2.1(a) and (b) shall be made in accordance with Code C, s. 11 if an authorised recording device in working order is not available (that is the case in this scenario) and (c) the 'relevant officer' described in para. 2.4 considers, on reasonable grounds, that the proposed interview or (as the case may be) continuation of the interview or other action, should not be delayed until an authorised recording device in working order and a suitable interview room or other location become available and decides that a written record shall be made. Paragraph 2.4(c)(i) states that in the case of a voluntary interview which takes place at a police station and the offence in question is an indictable offence, the 'relevant officer' means an officer of the rank of sergeant or above, in consultation with the investigating officer—therefore the answer is D and answers A, B and C are incorrect.

Investigators' Manual, para. 1.9.8

19. Answer **B** — Code D deals with the process of taking footwear impressions in connection with a criminal investigation. Impressions of a person's footwear may be taken in connection with the investigation of an offence only with their consent or if para. 4.17 applies. If the person is at a police station, consent must be in writing. Paragraph 4.17 states that s. 61A of PACE provides the power for a police officer to take footwear impressions without consent from any person over the age of 10 years who is detained at a police station:

(a) in consequence of being arrested for a recordable offence, or if the detainee has been charged with a recordable offence, or informed they will be reported for such an offence; and

(b) the detainee has not had an impression of their footwear taken in the course of the investigation of the offence unless the previously taken impression is not complete or is not of sufficient quality to allow satisfactory analysis, comparison or matching (whether in the case in question or generally).

This makes answers A and C incorrect (as the consent of OGINSKY or FARROW is not required). It is not necessary that the footprints are taken to prove or disprove the detained person's involvement in the offence, making answer D incorrect. Paragraph 4.18 of Code D states that reasonable force may be used, if necessary, to take a footwear impression from a detainee without consent under the power in para. 4.17 (correct answer B). A record must be made as soon as possible of the reason for taking a person's footwear impressions without consent. If force is used, a record shall be made of the circumstances and those present (Code D, para. 4.20).

Investigators' Manual, para. 1.8.5.3

20. Answer **A** — The doctrine of transferred *mens rea* is not restricted to offences under the Offences Against the Person Act 1861, making answer B incorrect. The issue of transferred *mens rea* can be important in relation to the liability of accessories. If the principal's intentions (BEST) are to be extended to an accessory (FLACK), it must be shown that those intentions were either contemplated and accepted by that person at the time of the offence, or that they were 'transferred'. So transferred *mens rea* is applicable to accessories and answer D is incorrect. An example is provided in the 2022 *Crime Manual* where a person (X) encourages another (Y) to assault Z. Y decides to attack a different person instead. X will not be liable for that assault because it was not contemplated or agreed by X. If, however, in trying to assault Z, Y happens to injure a third person inadvertently, then 'transferred *mens rea*' may result in X being liable for those injuries even though X had no wish for that person to be so injured. In trying to cause criminal damage to STIRLING's car, BEST damages a car owned by DUTTON—FLACK would be liable for that damage but would not be liable for the assault as that was not contemplated by FLACK so answer A is correct and answer C is incorrect.

Investigators' Manual, para. 1.2.11

21. Answer **A** — Answer D is incorrect as for the power under s. 32 to be lawfully used, the officer would have to have reasonable grounds for believing (not suspecting) that the arrested person may present a danger to themselves or others. Answer B is incorrect as the officer has a power under s. 32(2)(ii) to search the arrested person for anything which might be evidence relating to *an offence* (not just the offence for which the person was arrested). Answer C is incorrect as PC ARROW can search in PURLEY's mouth (see s. 32(4)). Answer A is the correct answer as trespassing on land with a firearm is a *summary only* offence. Section 32(2)(b) allows an officer to enter and search any premises where the offender was when arrested or immediately before for evidence relating to the offence but only if the offence for which he/she was arrested was *indictable*.

Investigators' Manual, para. 1.6.7

22. Answer **A** — A significant statement is one which appears capable of being used in evidence against the suspect, in particular a direct admission of guilt (Code C, para. 11.4A) and must have been made in the presence and hearing of a police officer (or other police staff member) (Code C, para. 11.4)—it could be made at any location (answer B is incorrect). Answer D is incorrect as a 'significant statement' will be made prior to a caution not after it. The suspect must be given the opportunity to clarify, confirm, deny or add to an earlier statement—the statement should be put to the suspect at the beginning of the interview, after caution and before questioning (answer C is incorrect).

Investigators' Manual, para. 1.9.3

23. Answer **C** — Section 3A(4) of the Bail Act 1976 states that where a custody officer has granted bail in criminal proceedings, he/she or *another custody officer* serving at the *same police station* may, at the request of the person to whom it was granted, vary the conditions of bail and in doing so he/she may impose conditions or more serious conditions, making answers A, B and D incorrect.

Investigators' Manual, para. 1.10.7.3

24. Answer **B** — Where a person is remanded in custody, it normally means detention in prison. However, s. 128 of the Magistrates' Courts Act 1980 provides that a magistrates' court may remand a person to police custody:

- for a period not exceeding three clear days (24 hours for persons under 18 (s. 91(5) of the Legal Aid, Sentencing and Punishment of Offenders Act 2012) (s. 128(7));
- for the purpose of enquiries into offences (other than the offence for which he/she appears before the court) (s. 128(8)(a));
- as soon as the need ceases, he/she must be brought back before the magistrates (s. 128(8)(b));
- the conditions of detention and periodic review apply as if the person was arrested without warrant on suspicion of having committed an offence (s. 128(8)(c) and (d)).

So FELL could be remanded in police custody for a period not exceeding three clear days and SAYER could be remanded in police custody for a period not exceeding 24 hours, meaning that answers A, C and D are incorrect.

Investigators' Manual, para. 1.10.10

25. Answer **A** — The relevant rank of an authorising officer for a CHIS is a superintendent and above. However, in urgent cases where it is not reasonably practicable to have the application considered by someone of that rank in the same organisation, an inspector may generally give the relevant authorisation (making answers C and D incorrect). Unless it is renewed, the authorisation given by a superintendent will ordinarily cease to have effect after 12 months, beginning on the day it was granted (Regulation of Investigatory Powers Act 2000, s. 43(3)(b)). If that authorisation was given orally by a superintendent in an urgent case, it will only last for 72 hours unless renewed and, where the case is urgent and the authority was given by an inspector, it will cease to have effect 72 hours later unless renewed (s. 43(3)(a)), making answer B incorrect. An authorisation by an inspector must be in writing.

Investigators' Manual, para. 1.12.3

26. Answer **C** — The Bail Act 1976, s. 6 creates two offences in relation to absconding and states:

(1) If a person who has been released on bail in criminal proceedings fails without reasonable cause to surrender to custody he shall be guilty of an offence.
(2) If a person who—
 (a) has been released on bail in criminal proceedings, and
 (b) having reasonable cause therefor, has failed to surrender to custody,

fails to surrender to custody at the appointed place as soon after the appointed time as is reasonably practicable he shall be guilty of an offence.

Answer B is incorrect as s. 6 applies where:

- the police grant bail to a suspect to appear at the police station;
- the police grant bail to a defendant to appear at court on the first appearance;
- the court grants bail to the defendant to return to court at a later date.

Answer B is further incorrect as in *Laidlaw* v *Atkinson* (1986) The Times, 2 August, it was held that being mistaken about the day on which one should have appeared was not a reasonable excuse. Answer D is incorrect as failure to give to a person granted bail in criminal proceedings a copy of the record of the decision does not constitute reasonable cause for that person's failure to surrender to custody (s. 6(4)). As these are not 'reasonable excuses', this makes answer C correct.

Investigators' Manual, para. 1.10.9

27. Answer **B** — Group identifications may take place either with the suspect's consent and co-operation or covertly without their consent, making answer A incorrect. Answer C is incorrect as group identifications can involve stationary or moving groups. If it is practicable, then the group identification process will be video recorded but this might not be possible (making answer D incorrect). Group identifications should only take place in police stations for reasons of safety, security or because it is not practicable to hold them elsewhere (correct answer B).

Investigators' Manual, para. 1.8.10

28. Answer **B** — Actions by the victim will sometimes be significant in the chain of causation, such as where a victim of a sexual assault was injured when jumping from her assailant's car (*R* v *Roberts* (1971) 56 Cr App R 95). Where such actions take place, the victim's behaviour *will not* necessarily be regarded as introducing a new intervening act. If the victim's actions are those which might reasonably be anticipated from any victim in such a situation, there will be no new and intervening act and the defendant will be responsible for the consequences flowing from them, meaning that answers A, C and D are incorrect.

Investigators' Manual, para. 1.3.6

29. Answer **C** — Code B, para. 3.4 states that applications for all search warrants must be made with the written authority of an officer of at least the rank of *inspector* (although in urgent cases where such an officer is not readily available, the most senior officer on duty may authorise the application), making answer A incorrect. Answer B is incorrect as s. 16(3) of PACE states that entry and search under such a warrant must be made within *three* months from the date of its issue. If the warrant is an all premises warrant, no premises which are not specified in it may be entered and searched unless a police officer of at least the rank of *inspector* has, in writing, authorised them to be entered (s. 16(3A)) making answer D incorrect.

Investigators' Manual, para. 1.6.4

30. Answer **D** — The Police and Criminal Evidence Act 1984, s. 18(1) states:

A constable may enter and search any premises *occupied or controlled* by a person who is under arrest for an indictable offence, if he has reasonable grounds for suspecting that there is on the premises evidence, other than items subject to legal privilege that relates—

(a) to that offence; or
(b) to some other indictable offence which is connected with or similar to that offence.

'Occupied or controlled' is highlighted as many persons believe that it states 'owns'. Reasonable suspicion that someone occupies or controls premises is not sufficient, making D the correct option.

Investigators' Manual, para. 1.6.7

31. Answer **A** — When a man calls another man 'mate' or 'lad', it is not demeaning. However, using words like 'chick, babes, bobs, honey, hun and sweetie' are all demeaning and infantilising ways of referring to women (*Hartley* v *D Hollowell & Sons Ltd* [2021] UKET Case No. 2405802/2020).

Investigators' Manual, para. 1.1.4.8

32. Answer **D** — In a case of simple criminal damage it may be relatively straightforward to prove a causal link between the actions of the defendant and the resulting crime: a defendant throws a brick at a window and the window is broken by the brick hitting it; the window would not have broken 'but for' the defendant's conduct. Where the link becomes more difficult to prove is when the defendant's behaviour triggers other events or aggravates existing circumstances. This MCQ is an example of such a situation and closely follows the circumstances of case law in the decision in *R* v *McKechnie* [1992] Crim LR 194. In that case, the defendant attacked the victim, who was already suffering from a serious ulcer, causing him brain damage. The brain damage (caused by the assault) prevented doctors from operating on the ulcer which eventually ruptured, killing the victim. The Court of Appeal, upholding the conviction for manslaughter, held that the defendant's criminal conduct (the assault) had made a significant contribution to the victim's death even though the untreated ulcer was the actual cause of death (correct answer D), therefore answers A and C are incorrect. Answer B is incorrect as the chain of causation can be broken, for example by an intervening act.

Investigators' Manual, para. 1.3.6

33. Answer **B** — Section 21A of the Criminal Procedure and Investigations Act 1996 introduced a Code of Practice for Arranging and Conducting Interviews of Witnesses Notified by the Accused. The Code sets out guidance that police officers and other persons charged with investigating offences must follow if they arrange or conduct interviews of proposed witnesses whose details are disclosed to the prosecution under the 1996 Act. If an investigator wishes to interview a witness, the witness must be asked whether they consent to being interviewed and informed that an interview is being requested following their identification by the accused as a proposed witness under s. 6A(2) or s. 6C of the Act and that they are not obliged to attend the proposed interview (correct answer B). The witness should be informed that they are entitled to be accompanied by a solicitor at the interview (making answer A incorrect) but nothing in this Code of Practice creates any duty on the part of the Legal Services Commission to provide funding for any such attendance (making answer C incorrect). Answer D is incorrect as there is no requirement for the interviewing officer to be of any specific rank.

Investigators' Manual, para. 1.11.11.7

34. Answer **A** — If an authorising officer, of superintendent rank or above, considers that access to a solicitor will interfere with evidence relating to an indictable offence, then access to that

solicitor may be delayed, making answer D incorrect. This authorisation to delay access is not a 'blanket' authorisation to deny access to all legal advisers and in the example given in the question, the authorising officer should consider offering the detained person access to another solicitor on the Duty Solicitor scheme, making answer C incorrect. The consultation with a solicitor must be in private (Code C, para. 6.1). In *Brennan* v *United Kingdom* (2001) 34 EHRR 507, the court held that a suspect's right to communicate confidentially with a solicitor 'is part of the basic requirements of a fair trial'. The court found that there had been a breach of Article 6(3)(c) because a police officer had been present during a suspect's first interview with his solicitor, making answer B incorrect.

Investigators' Manual, paras 1.7.11, 1.7.23

35. Answer **A** — The Police and Criminal Evidence Act 1984, s. 80 states:

(2A) In any proceedings the spouse or civil partner of a person charged in the proceedings shall, subject to subsection (4) below, be compellable—
  (a) to give evidence on behalf of any other person charged in the proceedings but only in respect of any specified offence with which that other person is charged; or
  (b) to give evidence for the *prosecution* but only in respect of any *specified offence* with which any person is charged in the proceedings.

(3) In relation to the spouse or civil partner of a person charged in any proceedings, an offence is a specified offence for the purposes of subsection (2A) above if—
  (a) it involves an assault on, or injury or a threat of injury to, the spouse or civil partner or a person who was at the material time under the age of 16;
  (b) it is a sexual offence alleged to have been committed in respect of a person who was at the material time under that age; or
  (c) it consists of attempting or conspiring to commit, or of aiding, abetting, counselling, procuring or inciting the commission of, an offence falling within paragraph (a) or (b) above.

The law in s. 80(2A) means that answer D is incorrect as a wife can be a compellable witness against her husband in relation to certain offences. Answer C is incorrect as the offence of murder in not contained in s. 80(3). In this situation, Felicity ABBOTT would not be a compellable witness. However, there is no requirement to tell a wife that she is not a compellable witness against her husband before interviewing her about a crime of which her husband is suspected (answer B is incorrect). A statement obtained from the wife in such circumstances could be admitted in evidence even though the wife refused to give evidence against her husband, provided it did not lead to an injustice (*R* v *L* [2008] EWCA Crim 973) (correct answer A).

Investigators' Manual, para. 1.5.7.5

36. Answer **D** — The first thing to consider here is Code E of the Codes of Practice. Paragraph 1.13 states:

Nothing in this Code requires the identity of officers or police staff conducting interviews to be recorded or disclosed if the interviewer reasonably believes recording or disclosing their name might put them in danger. In these cases, the officers and staff should use warrant or other identification numbers and the name of their police station. Such instances and the reasons for them shall be recorded in the custody record or the interviewer's pocket book.

This is relevant to visually recorded interviews where, at para. 2.7 of Code F we are told that:

In cases to which paragraph 1.13 of Code E (disclosure of identity of officers or police staff conducting interviews) applies:

(a) the officers and staff may have their backs to the visual recording device; and

(b) when in accordance with Code E paragraph 3.21 or 4.12 as they apply to this Code, arrangements are made for the suspect to have access to the visual recording, the investigating officer may arrange for anything in the recording that might allow the officers or police staff to be identified to be concealed.

Therefore answer D is correct and answers A, B and C are incorrect.

Investigators' Manual, paras 1.9.7, 1.9.13

37. Answer **B** — Section 16 of the Offences Against the Person Act 1861 states that a person who, without lawful excuse, makes to another a threat, intending that the other will fear that it will be carried out, to kill that other or a third person shall be guilty of an offence. The fact that WEIGHTMAN does not believe the threat is immaterial (making answer A incorrect). It can be committed via delivery of the threat to a third party (making answer C incorrect). It does not matter that the threat is made to kill at some time in the future—it is the intention to create the fear in the mind of another that is all important (making answer D incorrect).

Investigators' Manual, para. 2.7.8

38. Answer **D** — The Public Order Act 1986, s. 18 states:

(1) A person who uses threatening, abusive or insulting words or behaviour, or displays any written material which is threatening, abusive or insulting, is guilty of an offence if—
    (a) he intends thereby to stir up racial hatred, or
    (b) having regard to all the circumstances racial hatred is likely to be stirred up thereby.
(2) An offence under this section may be committed in a public or a private place, except that no offence is committed where the words or behaviour are used, or the written material is displayed, by a person inside a dwelling and are not heard or seen except by other persons in that or another dwelling [correct answer D].

Section 18(2) provides an exception to the offence, setting out circumstances where the offence *will not* be committed—this is the situation with BARTON—he *has not* committed the offence (answers A and C are incorrect). Answer B is incorrect as it can be committed by someone in a dwelling if the activity was heard or seen by a person who was not in the same dwelling or another one; for example, if a person walking on the street heard BARTON's language then the offence could be committed.

Investigators' Manual, para. 2.8.2.1

39. Answer **C** — 'Special defences' are only available to a defendant who is charged with an offence of murder—they cannot be used in answer to any other charge, e.g. attempted murder.

Investigators' Manual, para. 2.1.3.2

40. Answer **A** — Nobody is saying that WHYTE is guilty of an offence at this stage—this question simply asks 'Is he in possession of the cocaine?' and the answer is 'Yes' (answer A) because possession is a neutral concept, not implying any fault, blame or guilt. To be in 'possession' of something, the person needs to have custody/control of it and to know that the thing in question is under his/her control (making answer C incorrect). WHYTE knows he has custody/control over the envelope so he possesses it. It does not matter that he thinks it contains £200 cash or that he did not know that it contained cocaine (answers B and D)—he knew it contained something so he is therefore in possession of that something.

Investigators' Manual, paras 2.2.3 to 2.3.7

41. Answer **C** — Answers B and D are incorrect as a direction under s. 42 cannot be given as the Criminal Justice and Police Act 2001 gives the police specific powers to prevent the intimidation or harassment of people in *their own or others' homes* (correct answer C). Answer B is further incorrect as the direction does not have to be given by an officer in uniform. The direction is given by the most senior ranking police officer at the scene, making answer A incorrect.

Investigators' Manual, para. 2.8.7

42. Answer **A** — There is nothing preventing a charge of 'attempted kidnap', meaning that answer D is incorrect. The 'taking or carrying away' need not involve a great distance, meaning answer C is incorrect. Answer B is incorrect as the taking or carrying away can be accomplished by force or by fraud. In *R* v *Hendy-Freegard* [2007] EWCA Crim 1236, the defendant was a confidence trickster who pretended to be an undercover agent working for MI5 or Scotland Yard. He would tell his victims that he was investigating the activities of the IRA and that his investigations had revealed that they were in danger. This allowed him to take control of their lives for a number of years and in doing so to direct them to move about the country from location to location. The defendant was eventually arrested and convicted of kidnapping on the basis of the Crown's case that the offence of kidnapping had occurred, as his victims had made journeys around the country which they had been induced to make as a result of the defendant's false story. The defendant successfully appealed against the kidnapping conviction, with the court stating that causing a person to move from place to place *when unaccompanied by the defendant* could not itself constitute either taking or carrying away or deprivation of liberty, which were necessary elements of the offence.

Investigators' Manual, para. 2.11.3

43. Answer **B** — Under s. 1 of the Children and Young Persons Act 1933, an offence is committed when the offender 'neglects' a child. A person will be presumed to have neglected the child where it is proved that the child was an infant under 3 years old who died as a result of suffocation (other than by disease or blockage of the airways by an object) while in bed with someone of 16 years or over who was under the influence of drink or a prohibited drug when he/she went to bed or at any later time before the suffocation (s. 1(2)(b)). A drug is a prohibited drug for the purpose of s. 1(2)(b) in relation to a person if the person's possession of the drug immediately before taking it constituted an offence under s. 5(2) of the Misuse of Drugs Act 1971. This makes answers C and D incorrect.

Answer A is incorrect as the reference in s. 1(2)(b) to the infant being 'in bed' with another ('the adult') includes a reference to the infant lying next to the adult in or on any kind of furniture or surface being used by the adult for the purpose of sleeping (and the reference to the time when the adult 'went to bed' is to be read accordingly) (s. 1(2A)). A defendant may be charged with the above offence even where the child has died (s. 1(3)(b)) (correct answer B).

Investigators' Manual, para. 2.10.3

44. Answer **B** — The power to issue a Domestic Violence Protection Notice (a DVPN) is provided by s. 24 of the Crime and Security Act 2010, which states that a member of a police force not below the rank of superintendent ('the authorising officer') may issue a DVPN under this section (s. 24(1)). Before issuing a DVPN, the authorising officer must, in particular, consider several issues which includes any representations made by the person the notice is made in relation to (in this case, John EDMONSON) as to the issuing of the DVPN (correct answer B). Answer A is incorrect as a DVPN can be issued in circumstances where the person for whose protection it is issued does not consent to the issuing of the DVPN. Answer D is incorrect as the purpose of a DVPN is to secure the immediate protection of a victim of domestic violence and abuse (V) from future violence or a threat of violence from a suspected perpetrator (P). A DVPN prohibits P from molesting V and, where they cohabit, may require P to leave those premises. Where a DVPN has been issued, a constable (not the authorising officer) must apply to a magistrates' court for a Domestic Violence Protection Order (DVPO). The application must be heard by the magistrates' court not later than 48 hours (not 24) after the DVPN was served (s. 27) making answer C incorrect.

Investigators' Manual, para. 2.9.5

45. Answer **C** — The information of which NEWMAN is in possession would be classed as relating to 'terrorism' as defined in s. 1 of the Terrorism Act 2000. Answer A is incorrect as the disclosure of such information (in England and Wales) must be made to a constable not 'any person in authority'. Answer B is incorrect as s. 38B(6) of the Act means that a person resident in the United Kingdom could be charged with the offence even if he/she was outside the country when he/she became aware of the information. Answer D is incorrect as it is a defence for a person charged with such an offence to prove that he/she had a reasonable excuse for not making the disclosure (s. 38B(4)).

Investigators' Manual, para. 2.4.4.3

46. Answer **A** — Section 28 of the Violent Crime Reduction Act 2006 states:

(1) A person is guilty of an offence if—
  (a) he uses another to look after, hide or transport a dangerous weapon for him; and
  (b) he does so under arrangements or in circumstances that facilitate, or are intended to facilitate, the weapon's being available to him for an unlawful purpose.

(2) For the purposes of this section the cases in which a dangerous weapon is to be regarded as available to a person for an unlawful purpose include any case where—
  (a) the weapon is available for him to take possession of it at a time and place; and
  (b) his possession of the weapon at that time and place would constitute, or be likely to involve or to lead to, the commission by him of an offence.

It appears, on the face of it, that GLINSKI has committed the offence. However, a 'dangerous weapon' means a firearm other than an air weapon or a component part of, or accessory to, an air weapon; or a weapon to which s. 141 or 141A of the Criminal Justice Act 1988 applies. So whilst the offence does relate to firearms (making answer B incorrect), it does not relate to air weapons (making answers C and D incorrect).

Investigators' Manual, para. 2.3.9.6

47. Answer **D** — Section 1 of the Road Traffic Act 1988 states that a person who causes the death of another person by driving a mechanically propelled vehicle dangerously on a road or other public place is guilty of an offence. As the incident occurred on private land, the offence has not been committed (correct answer D). This immediately makes answers A and C incorrect as they are 'Yes' options but, in addition, answer A is incorrect as the fact that a driver was adversely affected by alcohol is a circumstance relevant to the issue of dangerous driving, but *is not* in itself determinative to prove the offence (*R* v *Webster* [2006] 2 Cr App R 103). Answer C is incorrect as stated, however it is relevant to point out that where the defendant is charged under s. 1, evidence of drink will be admissible where the quantity of it may have adversely affected the quality of the person's driving (*R* v *Woodward* [1995] RTR 130). Answer B states that the reason the offence has not been committed is that the death did not occur *while* VIVIER was driving but this is incorrect as the Court of Appeal has clarified that this offence relates to causing death *by* driving and not causing death *while* driving and therefore the 'driving' does not have to be coextensive with the collision that resulted in the death. In *R* v *Jenkins* [2012] EWCA Crim 2909, the court held that parking a van to make a delivery, leaving it in conditions of poor visibility where another vehicle collided with it, was certainly a causal link to the fatality that occurred.

Investigators' Manual, para. 2.14.5

48. Answer **C** — Section 17(2) states that if a person, at the time of his committing or being arrested for an offence specified in sch. 1 to this Act, has in his possession a firearm or imitation firearm, he shall be guilty of an offence under this subsection unless he shows that he had it in his possession for a lawful object. The offence applies to firearms and imitation firearms (so both the rifle and the imitation revolver would be covered), meaning that answer A is incorrect. Child abduction under s. 2 of the Child Abduction Act 1984 is a sch. 1 offence, meaning that answer B is incorrect. It does not matter whether the person concerned is ultimately found guilty of the offence for which they were arrested, making answer D incorrect.

Investigators' Manual, para. 2.3.9.5

49. Answer **A** — The Malicious Communications Act 1988, s. 1 states:

(1) Any person who sends to another person—
  (a) a letter, electronic communication or article of any description which conveys—
    (i) a message which is indecent or grossly offensive;
    (ii) a threat; or
    (iii) information which is false and known or believed to be false by the sender; or
  (b) any article or electronic communication which is, in whole or part, of an indecent or grossly offensive nature,

is guilty of an offence if his purpose, or one of his purposes, in sending it is that it should, so far as falling within paragraph (a) or (b) above, cause distress or anxiety to the recipient or to any other person to whom he intends that it or its contents or nature should be communicated.

The offence can be committed in a number of ways, not just by a threat (making answer B incorrect). Answer D is incorrect as the offence does not require a result—it is the 'purpose' (another way of saying 'intent') of the individual who sends the communication that is relevant. The offence is committed by a person who 'sends'—so when the communication is sent, the offence is complete (correct answer A) and this means that answer C is incorrect.

Investigators' Manual, para. 2.5.4

50. Answer **D** — 'Explosive substance' includes any materials for making any explosive substance; any implement or apparatus used, or intended or adapted to be used, for causing or aiding any explosion (s. 9(1)). The definition of 'explosive' under the Explosives Act 1875 also applies to this offence (*R* v *Wheatley* [1979] 1 WLR 144). Therefore fireworks and petrol bombs will be covered (*R* v *Bouch* [1983] QB 246). This means that answer A is incorrect. The Explosive Substances Act 1883, s. 4 states:

(1) Any person who makes or knowingly has in his possession or under his control any explosive substance under such circumstances as to give rise to a reasonable suspicion that he is not making it or does not have it in his possession or under his control for a lawful object, shall, unless he can show that he made it or had it in his possession or under his control for a lawful object, be guilty of [an offence] ...

The 'explosive substance' does not have to be made or possessed to cause injury only—it is about making or having it under your possession or control for a lawful object, making answer C incorrect. As the offence is about making, possession or control, CHALKLEY and McCABE commit the offence (correct answer D), making answer B incorrect.

Investigators' Manual, para. 2.4.8

51. Answer **C** — As this is an offence of intent, there is no need for a result to take place before the offence is complete, making answer D incorrect. Answer A is incorrect as the offence can be carried out for the benefit of anyone, including the person making the unauthorised access. The offences to which this offence applies are defined under s. 2(2) of the Act; STREET's activities *do not* constitute such an offence (making answer B incorrect). This is because he intends to steal *information* and this cannot be stolen as it is not property (*Oxford* v *Moss* (1978) 68 Cr App R 183) (see *Theft*, para. 3.1.7).

Investigators' Manual, para. 2.5.2.3

52. Answer **D** — Answer D is correct as this legislation covers the offence of common assault, or battery, when committed against an emergency worker acting in the exercise of functions as such a worker (including when an emergency worker is not at work but is carrying out the same activities as he/she would do at work).

Investigators' Manual, para. 2.7.6.2

53. Answer **B** — Answer C is incorrect as s. 5(4) of the Misuse of Drugs Act 1971 is a defence to unlawful possession—it will not provide a defence to any other offence connected with the

controlled drug (e.g. supplying or offering to supply). Answer D is incorrect as s. 28 is a general defence to a defendant charged with certain drugs offences. Section 28 applies to offences of:

- unlawful production (s. 4(2));
- unlawful supply (s. 4(3));
- unlawful possession (s. 5(2));
- possession with intent to supply (s. 5(3));
- unlawful cultivation of cannabis (s. 6(2));
- offences connected with opium (s. 9) (not covered in the NIE syllabus).

The defences under s. 28 are *not* available in cases of conspiracy as conspiracy is not an offence under the 1971 Act (*R* v *McGowan* [1990] Crim LR 399). Answer A is incorrect as possession of drugs paraphernalia (e.g. clingfilm, contact details etc.) will be relevant evidence to show that a defendant was an active dealer in drugs but it does not prove the intention to supply (*R* v *Haye* [2002] EWCA Crim 2476). In proving an intention to supply, you may be able to adduce evidence of the defendant's unexplained wealth (*R* v *Smith (Ivor)* [1995] Crim LR 940) or the presence of large sums of money with the drugs seized (*R* v *Wright* [1994] Crim LR 55) (correct answer B).

Investigators' Manual, paras 2.2.3.8, 2.2.5, 2.2.9

54. Answer **A** — Only one criminal damage offence is capable of being racially and/or religiously aggravated ('simple' criminal damage—Criminal Damage Act 1971, s. 1(1)) meaning that answer C is incorrect. Section 28 of the Crime and Disorder Act 1998 states:

(1) An offence is racially or religiously aggravated for the purposes of sections 29 to 32 . . . if—
  (a) at the time of committing the offence, or immediately before or after doing so, the offender demonstrates towards the victim of the offence hostility based on the victim's membership (or presumed membership) of a racial or religious group; or
  (b) the offence is *motivated (wholly or partly) by hostility* towards members of a racial or religious group based on their membership of that group.

As the offence was motivated by religious hostility, answer D is incorrect. A 'presumption' of racial/religious identity may well be wrong—that does not matter, so the fact that NORRIS is not from the religious group LEWIN presumed him to be does not stop the offence being committed therefore answer B is incorrect.

Investigators' Manual, paras 2.6.2 to 2.6.3.7

55. Answer **B** — The Public Order Act 1986, s. 29B states:

(1) A person who uses threatening words or behaviour, or displays any written material which is threatening, is guilty of an offence if he intends thereby to stir up religious hatred or hatred on the grounds of sexual orientation.
(2) An offence under this section is committed in a public or private place, except that no offence is committed where the words or behaviour are used, or the written material is displayed, by a person inside a dwelling and are not heard or seen except by other persons in that or another dwelling.

In proceedings for an offence under this section, it is a defence for the accused to prove that he/she was inside a dwelling and that he/she had no reason to believe that the words or behaviour used, or the written material displayed, would be heard or seen by a person outside that or any other dwelling.

These circumstances do not amount to an offence (correct answer B)—s. 29B(2) states that 'no offence is committed' when the written material is displayed by a person inside a dwelling (BERRY) and not seen except by other persons in that or another dwelling (KAPLAN). This means that answers A and C are incorrect—no offence has been committed. Answer D is incorrect as even if BERRY did intend to stir up religious hatred by displaying the flag, s. 29B(2) means that no offence is committed.

Investigators' Manual, para. 2.8.2.5

56. Answer **D** — Affray can take place in public or in private (making answer A incorrect). The offence does not require two or more persons to use or threaten to use unlawful violence (making answer B incorrect). Answer C is incorrect as affray can be committed by using or threatening to use unlawful violence. The House of Lords held that in order to prove the offence of affray, the threat of unlawful violence has to be towards a person(s) present at the scene (*I* v *DPP* [2001] UKHL 10). Once this element has been proved, it will be necessary to prove the second element; namely, whether the defendant's conduct would have caused a hypothetical person present at the scene to fear for his/her personal safety (*R* v *Sanchez* (1996) 160 JP 321 and *R* v *Carey* [2006] EWCA Crim 17). However, where the likelihood of a hypothetical person of reasonable firmness being present was low, this element of the offence was not satisfied. In *R (On the Application of Leeson)* v *DPP* [2010] EWHC 994 (Admin), a woman had issued a drunken threat to kill her long-term partner while holding a knife, in a bathroom in an otherwise unoccupied house. In these circumstances, the court held that there was no possibility of hypothetical bystanders fearing for their safety.

Investigators' Manual, para. 2.13.2

57. Answer **A** — Section 34(1) of the Policing and Crime Act 2009 states that a court may grant an injunction against a respondent aged 14 or over (making answer A correct). If an injunction is granted it will be because two conditions are met, the first being that the court is satisfied *on the balance of probabilities* that the respondent has engaged in or has encouraged or assisted gang-related violence, or gang-related drug-dealing activity (rather than beyond all reasonable doubt (incorrect answer B)). Section 34(5) states that for the purposes of this section, something is 'gang-related' if it occurs in the course of, or is otherwise related to, the activities of a group that consists of at least three (not five—incorrect answer C) people, and has one or more characteristics that enable its members to be identified by others as a group. The court *may* attach a power of arrest in relation to any prohibition in the injunction or any requirement in the injunction *other than* one which has the effect of requiring the respondent to participate in particular activities (s. 36) (incorrect answer D).

Investigators' Manual, para. 2.12.2

58. Answer **D** — A common assault by battery (beating) involves the actual use of force by an assailant on a victim but which only results in very minor or no perceivable injury. It is the intentional or reckless application of force on another and can range from a push to a punch,

and depends on how much harm is done and the injury received. The application of force can be carried out indirectly—the circumstances of the question are such an example where injury is caused to the baby by BOTHAM punching ZAPPE who drops the baby to the ground causing slight injury. This is a s. 39 offence (a battery) meaning that answers B and C are eliminated. The offence under s. 47 of the Offences Against the Person Act 1861 (Actual Bodily Harm (ABH)) is exactly the same as a s. 39 offence but can be distinguished from s. 39 by the degree of injury. *R* v *Donovan* [1934] 2 KB 498 at 509, [1934] All ER Rep 207 suggested that 'bodily harm has its ordinary meaning' and includes 'any hurt or injury calculated to interfere with the health or comfort of the victim. Such hurt or injury need not be permanent, but must, no doubt, be more than merely transient and trifling.' A momentary loss of consciousness has been held to be 'actual harm' (*R* v *Miller*; *T* v *DPP* [2003] EWHC 266 (Admin))—the significant bruising is just that, 'significant', and amounts to more than transient/trifling harm (ABH) therefore a charge of s. 47 would be appropriate in this situation, making answer A incorrect.

Investigators' Manual, paras 2.7.3, 2.7.6.1, 2.7.6.3

59. Answer **A** — The Criminal Damage Act 1971, s. 1 states:

(1) A person who without lawful excuse destroys or damages any property belonging to another intending to destroy or damage any such property or being reckless as to whether any such property would be destroyed or damaged shall be guilty of an offence.

A person shall be treated as having lawful excuse under s. 5(2):

(a) if at the time of the act or acts alleged to constitute the offence he believed that the person or persons whom he believed to be entitled to consent to the destruction of or damage to the property in question had so consented, or would have so consented to it if he or they had known of the destruction or damage and its circumstances ...

That would be the case in respect of ORTEGA as s. 5(2)(a) would provide a statutory defence to any later charge of criminal damage by Amy SAMUELSON. The key element here would be that ORTEGA believed she had the consent of the owner of the TV (Kelly SAMUELSON and someone ORTEGA believes to be entitled to consent to that damage) to damage the TV in these circumstances. This makes answers B and C incorrect.

Section 10 of the Act deals with the 'belonging to another' phrase and states:

(2) Property shall be treated for the purposes of this Act as belonging to any person—
  (a) having the custody or control of it;
  (b) having in it any proprietary right or interest (not being an equitable interest arising only from an agreement to transfer or grant an interest); or
  (c) having a charge on it.

This extended meaning of 'belonging to another' is similar to that used in the Theft Act 1968. One result is that if a person damages their own property, they may still commit the offence of simple criminal damage if that property also 'belongs to' someone else. As Kelly knows this is the case, she could be charged with criminal damage (making answer C further incorrect). Answer D is incorrect as the Theft Act 1968 states that where the property in question belongs to D's spouse or civil partner, a prosecution for unlawful damage may only be instituted against D by or with the consent of the DPP (s. 30(4)). This restriction does not apply to other persons charged with committing the offence jointly with D; nor does it apply when the parties are separated by judicial decree or order or under no obligation to cohabit (s. 30(4)(a)).

Investigators' Manual, paras 3.9.2 to 3.9.2.5

60. Answer **B** — Any representation made must be one as to fact or law, so a broken promise is not in itself a false representation. However, a statement may be false if it misrepresents the current intentions or state of mind of the person making it or anyone else. This MCQ is a good example of such behaviour. CROFTON visits WOODWARD's house and tells WOODWARD that he needs emergency work carried out on his roof. CROFTON states that he is in a position to do the work immediately but only if WOODWARD pays him £150 there and then. WOODWARD gives CROFTON the money and CROFTON then leaves without carrying out the work; the truth of the matter is that CROFTON had never intended to carry out the work. Such a 'promise' by CROFTON would amount to an offence as it involved a false representation, i.e. he never intended to keep the promise (this makes answer A incorrect). Answer D is incorrect as the offence is complete the moment the false representation is made. Answer C is incorrect as the mode of trial for the fraud offence is not related to the value of the goods concerned (in a way that you might associate with low-value shoplifting).

Investigators' Manual, paras 3.7.2 to 3.7.4

61. Answer **B** — There are two forms of burglary—s. 9(1)(a) and s. 9(1)(b). The Theft Act 1968, s. 9 states:

(1) A person is guilty of burglary if—
  (a) he enters any building or part of a building as a trespasser and with intent to commit any such offence as is mentioned in subsection (2) below; or ...
(2) The offences referred to in subsection (1)(a) above are offences of stealing anything in the building or part of a building in question, of inflicting on any person therein any grievous bodily harm and of doing unlawful damage to the building or anything therein.

The s. 9(1)(a) offence is committed at one point only—the point of entry. The necessary intention must be in the mind of the defendant at that time and at no stage does BARKER ever 'enter' with intent so there is no offence under s. 9(1)(a) to consider at any stage.

The Theft Act 1968, s. 9 states:

(1) A person is guilty of burglary if—
  (b) having entered any building or part of a building as a trespasser he steals or attempts to steal anything in the building or that part of it or inflicts or attempts to inflict on any person therein any grievous bodily harm.

BARKER has entered the warehouse as a trespasser when he breaks in looking for shelter but when he turns on the electric fire to warm himself up this is not 'stealing' as electricity is not 'property' for the purposes of the offence of theft, so no burglary is committed at point A. However, when he steals the £30 cash he does commit a s. 9(1)(b) offence (answer B is the correct answer as the question asks when a burglary is first committed). There is no burglary at point C (this is criminal damage)—a further burglary under s. 9(1)(b) is committed when BARKER steals the batteries (point D).

Investigators' Manual, paras 3.4.1 to 3.4.5

62. Answer **D** — A commits an offence when he/she is in *possession or control* of articles for use in a fraud (s. 6 of the Fraud Act 2006), not 'with him/her' making answer A incorrect. The articles can be anything at all (the blank credit cards and the skimming machine) and also include a computer program or data held in electronic form—so all of the articles are covered. For possession, the person must have immediate physical control over the article and know that it is there. Having control would include having physical control at a distance and also knowing that the article was there. This offence can be committed anywhere, including when the articles are located in the suspect's home. This makes answer B incorrect. As all the articles are covered, the correct answer is D (answer C is incorrect).

Investigators' Manual, para. 3.7.7

63. Answer **A** — Section 27 of the Theft Act 1968 allows for the admissibility of previous misconduct and states:

    (3) Where a person is being proceeded against for handling stolen goods (but not for any offence other than handling stolen goods), then at any stage of the proceedings, if evidence has been given of his having or arranging to have in his possession the goods the subject of the charge, or of his undertaking or assisting in, or arranging to undertake or assist in, their retention, removal, disposal or realisation, the following evidence shall be admissible for the purpose of proving that he knew or believed the goods to be stolen goods—
    (a) evidence that he has had in his possession, or has undertaken or assisted in the retention, removal, disposal or realisation of, stolen goods from any theft taking place not earlier than 12 months before the offence charged; and
    (b) (provided that seven days' notice in writing has been given to him of the intention to prove the conviction) evidence that he has within the five years preceding the date of the offence charged been convicted of theft or of handling stolen goods.

    Therefore DUBAR's previous conviction and the evidence that he had stolen property in his possession nine months before the handling offence he is charged with are admissible, making answers B, C and D incorrect.

Investigators' Manual, para. 3.6.6

64. Answer **C** — Robbery is committed when a person steals and immediately before or at the time of doing so, and in order to do so, they use force on any person or put or seek to put any person in fear of being then and there subjected to force. What this means is that when force is threatened the person being threatened must fear force for *him/herself and not for another*. So when the gun is pointed towards the back of the customer, the cashier cannot fear force on the customer's behalf meaning that at points A and B no offence of robbery has been committed.

    When force is used, it can be used on *anyone* in order to commit the theft. So when CLARKE hits the customer, force is being used on *any person* in order to commit a theft. When the cashier hands over the money, at that point the offence of robbery is complete, making answer D incorrect.

Investigators' Manual, para. 3.2.1

65. Answer **D** — Under s. 4(2) of the Theft Act 1968, you cannot generally steal land; however, there are exceptions to this rule. Things growing wild on any land (in this case, the raspberries growing on land belonging to FISHER) are 'property' and could be stolen by a person not in possession of the land (KOWALSKI) if he/she severed and appropriated them. However, s. 4(3) of the Act tells us that a person who picks mushrooms, flowers, fruit and foliage growing wild on any land will not commit theft by so doing unless the picking is done for reward, sale or other commercial purpose; therefore, KOWALSKI does not commit theft in relation to the raspberries making answers A and C incorrect. Section 4(2)(c) states that theft can be committed by a tenant when that tenant appropriates the whole or part of any fixture or structure let to be used with the land. Examples of 'fixtures' would be a fireplace or a kitchen sink; a structure might be a greenhouse or a garden shed which is fixed to the land. A tenant cannot steal land such as topsoil or a lilac tree growing in the garden of the rented premises as these things are not 'fixtures or structures', making answer B incorrect.

Investigators' Manual, para. 3.1.5

66. Answer **C** — To commit a s. 9(1)(a) burglary, the offender must enter a building or part of a building as a trespasser with the intention of stealing anything therein, committing grievous bodily harm or criminal damage—DOOLEY had none of these intentions so a s. 9(1)(a) offence is not committed, making answer A incorrect. Answer B is incorrect as an aggravated burglary is an aggravated version of the s. 9(1)(a) offence or the s. 9(1)(b) offence. We have established that DOOLEY has not committed a s. 9(1)(a) offence and that remains the case when he enters the lounge. As a s. 9(1)(a) can only be committed at the point of entry, no aggravated s. 9(1)(a) has been committed. Inside the lounge, he can only commit a s. 9(1)(b) burglary—having entered a building or part of a building as a trespasser, he steals or attempts to steal, commits or attempts to commit grievous bodily harm. He has not done anything that fits the s. 9(1)(b) offence so when he picks up the poker, this is not a burglary. However, when he picks up the poker he decides to use it to cause grievous bodily harm and at that stage the poker becomes a weapon of offence (instant arming). When he moves from the lounge into the hallway, he enters part of a building (the hallway) as a trespasser and at that stage he intends to cause LOW grievous bodily harm—this is a s. 9(1)(a) burglary. At the time of the s. 9(1)(a), he has with him a weapon of offence and consequently commits an aggravated burglary at that stage (answer C) making answer D incorrect.

Investigators' Manual, paras 3.4.1 to 3.5.1

67. Answer **A** — Robbery is committed when a person steals and, immediately before or at the time of doing so and in order to do so, they use force on any person or put or seek to put any person in fear of being then and there subjected to force. However, there must be a theft for a robbery to occur ('and thief and steal shall be construed accordingly'). If there is no theft, then there is no robbery. Here there is no theft because PUGH honestly believes that he has a lawful right to deprive CANNON of the property. The circumstances of the question are very similar to the case of *R* v *Robinson* [1977] Crim LR 173, where D, who was owed £7 by P's wife, approached P, brandishing a knife. A fight followed, during which P dropped a £5 note.

D picked it up and demanded the remaining £2 owed to him. Allowing D's appeal against a conviction for robbery, the Court of Appeal held that the prosecution had to prove that D was guilty of theft, and that he would not be (under s. 2(1)(a) of the Theft Act 1968) if he believed that he had a right in law to deprive P of the money, even though he knew that he was not entitled to use the knife to get it, i.e. there was no dishonesty. The fact that PUGH knows the means he is using are wrong does not alter the dishonesty element.

Investigators' Manual, para. 3.2.1

68. Answer **A** — The offence of aggravated burglary under s. 10 of the Theft Act is committed when a person commits a burglary (under s. 9(1)(a) or s. 9(1)(b)) and at the time has with him/her any firearm, imitation firearm, any weapon of offence or any explosive. A weapon of offence is any article made, adapted or intended to cause injury to another or to incapacitate another. A bayonet is a weapon of offence per se and the rope is a weapon of offence as KELT intends to use it to incapacitate a person. The phrase 'has with him' means 'immediate control of the item'. As KELT *knows* about the bayonet then he 'has it with him'. This means that CALDERDALE and KELT commit the offence in relation to the bayonet (answer D is incorrect) but only KELT in relation to the rope (making answers B and C incorrect and answer A correct).

Investigators' Manual, para. 3.5.1

69. Answer **B** — Rape is committed when a person (A) intentionally penetrates the vagina, anus or mouth of another person (B) with his penis and B does not consent to the penetration and A does not reasonably believe B consents. A central element to the offence is the absence of consent (s. 74 of the Act) which states that a person consents if he/she agrees by choice and has the freedom and capacity to make that choice. In this situation, 'true' consent has been given so the offence has not been committed. Section 75 of the Act enables a court to presume that the victim did not consent if evidence presented in court proves that the circumstances involved any of the following: use of or fear of immediate violence against that or another person; unlawful detention; unconsciousness; inability to communicate due to physical disability; and/or substances that are capable of stupefying or overpowering (such as drugs) were non-consensually administered. It also has to be proved that the defendant knew of these circumstances and that the defendant carried out the act in question. Purely because violence was not used or threatened would not mean that a person consented to the relevant activity (answer D is incorrect). BUCKINGHAM may have lied about his wealth and the promise to marry but those lies were not about the nature or purpose of the relevant act, so answers A and C are incorrect.

Investigators' Manual, paras 4.2.1 to 4.2.6

70. Answer **A** — Answer C is incorrect as a 'relevant sexual offence' means an offence under Part I of the Sexual Offences Act 2003 (virtually all regularly occurring sexual offences) including aiding, abetting, counselling or procuring such an offence (s. 62(2)). Answer B is incorrect as the offence could cover any situation from the theft of drugs or equipment to be used in the course of the sexual offence and going equipped for burglary, to the taking of a vehicle or even dangerous driving with the intention in each case of committing the further relevant sexual offence. Answer D is incorrect as if A does commit the intended offence, he/she could be charged with the substantive sexual offence in addition to this offence (correct answer A).

Investigators' Manual, para. 4.6.2

71. Answer **A** — Under s. 3 of the Sexual Offences Act 2003, a person commits an offence if he intentionally touches another person (B), the touching is sexual, B does not consent to the touching and A does not reasonably believe that B consents. It does not have to involve touching the genitals (answer B is incorrect). 'Touching' includes (but is not limited to) touching with any part of the body (answer D is incorrect), with anything else or through anything else (e.g. clothing). The offence does not require that the activity is carried out for sexual gratification (answer C is incorrect).

Investigators' Manual, paras 4.3.3 to 4.3.4

72. Answer **B** — The Sexual Offences Act 2003, s. 1 states:

(1) A person (A) commits an offence if—
  (a) he intentionally penetrates the vagina, anus or mouth of another person (B) with his penis,
  (b) B does not consent to the penetration, and
  (c) A does not reasonably believe that B consents.

A person consents if they agree by choice, and have the freedom and capacity to make that choice (s. 74 of the Act)—any consent given must be 'true' consent, not simply a *submission* induced by fear or fraud. Therefore, if the person does not have any real choice in the matter, or the choice is not a genuine exercise of free will, then he/she has not 'consented'. Obtaining consent by fear or force would not be 'true consent' but if consent has been obtained by other means it does not automatically mean that the person consented (answer C is incorrect). ROE did consent to having sexual intercourse with HANRAHAN but her consent was given with the express condition that HANRAHAN would wear a condom—he did put on a condom but then took it off and this would amount to an offence of rape (answer A is incorrect). The question is closely associated to the case law decision in *Assange* v *Sweden* [2011] EWHC 2489 (Admin). In this case, the Divisional Court considered the situation in which A knew that B (the complainant) would only consent to sexual intercourse if he used a condom. The court rejected the view that the conclusive presumption in s. 76 of the Sexual Offences Act 2003 would apply (answer D is incorrect) and concluded that the issue of consent could be determined under s. 74 rather than s. 76 (correct answer B), and stated that it would be open to a jury to hold that if B had made it clear that she would only consent to sexual intercourse if A used a condom, then there would be no consent if, without B's consent, A did not use a condom or removed or tore the condom. A's conduct in having sexual intercourse without a condom in circumstances where B had made it clear that she would only have sexual intercourse if A did use a condom, would therefore amount to an offence.

Investigators' Manual, paras 4.2.1 to 4.2.7

73. Answer **D** — The offence under s. 15 cannot be committed by a person under 18.

Investigators' Manual, para. 4.4.8

74. Answer **A** — Section 3 of the Sexual Offences Act 2003 states that a person (A) commits an offence if he/she intentionally touches another person (B) and the touching is sexual and B does not consent to the touching and A does not reasonably believe that B consents. 'Touching' includes (but is not limited to) touching with any part of the body, with anything else or through anything else (using a newspaper to touch a person's breasts), so answers B and D are

incorrect. The presumptions under s. 75 would be applicable to this offence (so answer C is incorrect) and would be relevant (the threat of immediate violence).

Investigators' Manual, paras 4.3.3 to 4.3.4

75. Answer **D** — The Sexual Offences Act 2003, s. 30 states:

(1) A person (A) commits an offence if—
   (a) he intentionally touches another person (B),
   (b) the touching is sexual,
   (c) B is unable to refuse because of or for a reason related to a mental disorder, and
   (d) A knows or could reasonably be expected to know that B has a mental disorder and that because of it or for a reason related to it B is likely to be unable to refuse.

A person is unable to refuse if:

- he/she lacks the capacity to choose whether to agree to the touching (whether because of a lack of sufficient understanding of the nature or reasonably foreseeable consequences of what is being done, or for any other reason); or
- he/she is unable to communicate such a choice to the defendant (s. 30(2)).

The age of the offender and victim are immaterial to this offence (answer A is incorrect). Penetration is not required (answer C is incorrect). Answer B is incorrect as there is no requirement for sexual gratification. You must show that the defendant knew or could reasonably have been expected to know both that the victim had a mental disorder and that, because of it (or for a reason related to it), he/she was likely to be unable to refuse (that is certainly the case with BRANNIGAN). In *Hulme* v *DPP* [2006] EWHC 1347 (Admin), the Divisional Court examined a decision reached by a magistrates' court in relation to a complainant who was a cerebral palsy sufferer with a low IQ (aged 27). The magistrates' court had decided that the complainant was unable to refuse to be touched sexually; the Divisional Court agreed and the conviction against the defendant (who was 73) was upheld (the correct answer is therefore D).

Investigators' Manual, para. 4.5.3

76. Answer **C** — For the s. 11 offence, the offender must know or believe that the child is under 16 (so answer D is incorrect). The activity in which the offender is engaged must be 'sexual' and intentional and must be in order to obtain sexual gratification (for the defendant—not the victim)—answer A is incorrect. It does not have to be carried out in the 'physical presence' of the victim so answer B is incorrect. However, the victim does not actually have to be aware of the activity (e.g. if the child does not notice).

Investigators' Manual, para. 4.4.2

77. Answer **D** — The Sexual Offences Act 2003, s. 12 states:

(1) A person aged 18 or over (A) commits an offence if—
   (a) for the purpose of obtaining sexual gratification, he intentionally causes another person (B) to watch a third person engaging in an activity, or to look at an image of any person engaging in an activity,
   (b) the activity is sexual, and

(c) either—
    (i) B is under 16 and A does not reasonably believe B is 16 or over, or
    (ii) B is under 13.

The issue here is whether NELSON committed the offence and if so at what point it was *first* committed. He knows her to be under 16 and the showing of the images and pictures was for sexual gratification. He can commit the offence by achieving sexual gratification from her watching of the images but, in this question, this was not the case. His motive was to lower the victim's inhibitions. Therefore he commits the offence when he first shows the first image. Image includes a moving or still image and includes an image produced by any means and, where the context permits, a three-dimensional image and it also includes an image of an imaginary person. It does not follow that the sexual gratification has to be immediate, i.e. simultaneous, contemporaneous or synchronised, it can be to put the child in the frame of mind for future sexual abuse (*R* v *Abdullahi* [2006] EWCA Crim 2060), making D the correct answer.

Investigators' Manual, para. 4.4.5

78. Answer **B** — The Sexual Offences (Amendment) Act 1992 provides anonymity to a victim/complainant of most sexual offences. It applies to almost all sexual offences under Part 1 of the Sexual Offences Act 2003 (such as rape, assault by penetration, sexual assault by touching etc.) *as well as attempts* and conspiracy to commit such acts. It also applies to aiding, abetting, counselling or procuring any of these offences (making answers A and D incorrect). The alleged victim/complainant is entitled to anonymity *throughout their lifetime* (making answer C incorrect). Once an allegation of one of the offences in question has been made, nothing may be published which is likely to lead members of the public to identify the alleged victim/complainant. The protection under s. 1(2) applies from the time someone is accused for that person's lifetime even if proceedings are later abandoned (correct answer B).

Investigators' Manual, para. 4.1.2

79. Answer **A** — The Sexual Offences Act 2003, s. 2 states:

(1) A person (A) commits an offence if—
    (a) he intentionally penetrates the vagina or anus of another person (B) with a part of his body or anything else,
    (b) the penetration is sexual,
    (c) B does not consent to the penetration, and
    (d) A does not reasonably believe that B consents.

The victim's vagina and/or anus was not penetrated by ALLSOPP and GREY so the offence under s. 2 has not been committed (correct answer A).

Investigators' Manual, para. 4.3.1

80. Answer **C** — The Sexual Offences Act 2003, s. 61 states:

(1) A person commits an offence if he intentionally administers a substance to, or causes a substance to be taken by, another person (B)—
    (a) knowing that B does not consent, and

(b) with the intention of stupefying or overpowering B, so as to enable *any person* to engage in a sexual activity that involves B.

Section 61(b) rules out answer B as being the correct option (the substance is administered to enable *any person* to engage in sexual activity).

This offence is aimed at the use of 'date rape' drugs administered without the victim's knowledge or consent but would also cover the use of any other substance with the relevant intention. It would cover GREENFIELD spiking CAVANAH's soft drink with alcohol where CAVANAH did not know she was consuming alcohol (making answer A incorrect). This offence applies both when A him/herself administers the substance to B, and where A causes the substance to be taken by B, for example when A persuades a friend (C) to administer a substance to B, so that A can have sex with B because C knows B socially and can more easily slip the substance into B's drink than A (making MILLER and GREENFIELD guilty of the offence) so answer D is incorrect and answer C is correct.

Investigators' Manual, para. 4.6.1